When Love Ends

and the Ice Cream Carton Is Empty

What You Need to Know about Your New Beginning

Jackie M. Johnson

MOODY PUBLISHERS

CHICAGO

All Scripture quotations, unless otherwise indicated, are taken from the *Holy Bible, New International Version®*. NIV®. Copyright © 1973, 1978, 1984 by Biblica, Inc.™ Used by permission of Zondervan. All rights reserved.

Scripture quotations marked NKJV are taken from the *New King James Version*. Copyright © 1982 by Thomas Nelson, Inc. Used by permission. All rights reserved.

Scripture quotations marked NLT are taken from the *Holy Bible, New Living Translation*, copyright 1996, 2004. Used by permission of Tyndale House Publishers, Inc., Wheaton, Illinois 60189. All rights reserved.

Scripture quotations marked NASB are taken from the *New American Standard Bible®*, copyright ©1960, 1962, 1963, 1968, 1971, 1972, 1973, 1975, 1977, 1995 by The Lockman Foundation. Used by permission. (www.Lockman.org)

Scripture quotations marked MSG or *The Message* are taken from *The Message*. Copyright © 1993, 1994, 1995, 1996, 2000, 2001, 2002, 2003 by Eugene H. Peterson. Used by permission of NavPress Publishing Group.

The names of the people in the stories listed in this book have been changed.

Editor: Jocelyn Green
Interior Design: Ragont Design
Cover and Image Design: John Hamilton Design

Library of Congress Cataloging-in-Publication Data

Johnson, Jackie M.
 When love ends and the ice cream carton is empty : what you need to know about your new beginning / Jackie M. Johnson.
  p. cm.
Includes bibliographical references.
ISBN 978-0-8024-8352-2
1. Single women--Religious life. 2. Rejection (Psychology)--Religious aspects--Christianity. 3. Dating (Social customs)--Religious aspects--Christianity. I. Title.
BV4596.S5J23 2010
248.8'432--dc22
                                        2009053297

We hope you enjoy this book from Moody Publishers. Our goal is to provide high-quality, thought-provoking books and products that connect truth to your real needs and challenges. For more information on other books and products written and produced from a biblical perspective, go to www.moodypublishers.com or write to:

Moody Publishers
820 N. LaSalle Boulevard
Chicago, IL 60610

1 3 5 7 9 10 8 6 4 2

Printed in the United States of America

Also by Jackie M. Johnson

Power Prayers for Women

*This book is dedicated
to those who have the courage to believe
that God redeems loss and pain
and heals the heart to love again.*

Contents

Introduction

Though I sit in darkness, the Lord will be my light.
—Micah 7:8

Breakups are hard. Whether you're trying to get over someone who left or you're the one leaving, breakups are messy, complicated, and often devastatingly difficult. That's because we're designed for attachment and connection, not separation and disconnection. Yet, for many singles, our dating lives are a series of hellos and good-byes—attaching and detaching—from our teenage years until we stand at the altar (or don't). We date and break up, date and break up in a crazy-making cycle. Often, people who marry and divorce find themselves back in the same pattern, too.

Whether you dated briefly or for a long time, the loss of love can be shattering. Your mind swirls with questions: *What did I do wrong? Why did he leave? Aren't I worth being loved well? What if I never find anyone like him again? What if I never find anyone again?*

One day you're sad, the next day you're angry, and suddenly you're just numb; you don't feel anything because it just hurts too much to feel. Maybe you feel rejected, betrayed, or broken-hearted. If you're the one who left him, you may be suffering guilt and shame. Either way, you just want the pain to stop. You want healing and you want answers.

Is it possible to get through this fragmenting process without falling to pieces?

Yes. Thankfully, yes.

If you've just broken up from a dating relationship, or are still in the process, *When Love Ends* is an excellent resource. It provides encouragement and hope along with biblical insight and practical help to get you out of the darkness and back into the light of a brighter future.

Every story has a beginning and an end. This book begins with an ending, the "heart sunset" of your fading relationship, and it ends with a fresh start in the land of new beginnings.

When Love Ends is an integral part of your healing journey. In this four-part book, you'll follow the cycle of a day, from darkness to light, as an analogy that parallels the healing process.

Twilight is a time of endings. The sun and the relationship are both disappearing, and you learn that, sadly, loss and brokenness are a part of life. Yet *how* you deal with endings, how you handle the emotional fallout of your breakup, in healthy or unhealthy ways, will determine the quality of your future love relationships—and your life.

Night is about healing emotional pain. You've lost love, friendship, physical touch, and the hope of being with this person forever. You seem to have misplaced your worth and value, and your self-esteem is in hiding. Repairing heartache comes as you learn to process your emotions and discover some essential keys to healing the hurt. With the "night lights" God provides during life's dark times, like His comfort, wisdom, and unconditional love, you are well on your way toward the daylight of joy.

As the first fingers of morning inch across the horizon, the light of *Dawn* awakens hope. You begin to understand more about God's character and how He redeems losses and restores brokenness. Illumination brings restoration, and as you discover your true identity as a dearly loved child of God, you gain greater confidence and learn to make wiser choices in love.

Finally *Day* breaks and you find that letting go of the past is truly possible. It's time to move forward into your future. As the sun's rays shine into the dark corners of your life, you reawaken to important things you've forgotten or put aside, like: gratitude, serving others, building friendships and community, and maybe even living your dreams. With renewed vision, you are no longer hiding in the shadows of yesterday. Radiance has returned, and with the light of Christ in you, you are ready to be a light to the world.

One of the most important things you will encounter on your expedition from breaking up to beginning again is learning to grieve—to process emotions, not avoid them, stuff them, or handle them in unhealthy or destructive ways. Doing so is essential to moving forward.

In fact, unresolved grief blocks our emotions from being heart-healthy in the area of relationships. When you deal with emotional wounds and let God heal them, you can be better equipped to find the healthy and lasting love you truly desire.

However, to cope with the emotional rubble from a broken heart, many of us turn to our favorite comfort foods—like ice cream, potato chips, chocolate, creamy mashed potatoes, or fresh, hot bread slathered in butter—to try and fill the emptiness and soothe the sorrow. Others lose their appetite completely.

Could it be that your comfort choice has gone down a darker path, like drinking away your pain, taking drugs, or having sex with someone you're not married to—another Mr. Wrong just to try to feel good about yourself for just a little while?

Others, like my friend Alice, turn to books for comfort. She loves to snuggle up with a cozy blanket and a cup of hot tea to read a good book that meets her right where she's at—and that's what I hope this book will do for you. Comfort, yes, but so much more. *When Love Ends* is a heart-healing journey that will lead you from the darkness of your breakup pain and into the light of brighter and better days ahead.

In the long run, comfort food in moderation isn't going to hurt you, but it's not going to heal your broken heart. It may seem to satisfy you for a time, but the void remains—the heart holes of loss, loneliness, rejection or regret. What are you going to do to get past the pain when the pint or plate of food is empty?

HEAL YOUR HEART, CHANGE YOUR LIFE

It's time to put down the ice cream carton and pick up your Bible—and this book—to get through the sadness, past the pain, and back into joy, life, and love again. *When Love Ends* is not just about healing your heart, it's about changing your life.

Do you need comfort and support to cope with your disappointment? Do you want to get unstuck and move forward with your life? If so, read on.

God heals brokenness; He redeems loss and pain and heals the heart to love again. He is all about restoration and transformation—from sadness to joy, from rejection to acceptance, and from brokenness to wholeness. The One who loves you most can help you reconnect again—to Himself, yourself, and others—and in the process to discover what real, healthy love looks like so you can make wiser choices next time.

Each chapter in *When Love Ends* includes a short healing prayer and discussion questions for use with a small group or Bible study, or for your own personal use. Day by day, step by step, and choice by choice, healing comes. The good news is that despite your soul injuries, you can live a full and joyful life. It may feel like "The End," but your new beginning will come.

Nightfall is approaching. But you don't have to be afraid of the dark, for you are not alone. Not ever. Even in the diffused light of dusk, when you can hardly see the way, God's lantern of truth and His presence remain constant. He will be with you through the night and lead you to hope, healing, and brighter days ahead.

You just have to follow the Light.

Part 1: Twilight

1 Sunset: Dealing with Endings

There is a time for everything, and a season
for every activity under heaven . . .
a time to tear and a time to mend.
—Ecclesiastes 3:1, 7

Twilight is a time of transition. As late afternoon fades into evening, the vivid colors of day disappear, and the sun, low in the horizon, dips slowly into earth's edge. In the dimness before nightfall it becomes increasingly hard to see. Soon it will be dark. Likewise, a relationship ending is your own "heart sunset." Good-bye day; good-bye love.

WHY BREAKUPS HAPPEN

As early evening settles in, dusk becomes an ambiguous zone. With less light, things can seem uncertain or unclear, like why your relationship ended. Sometimes you are left without the answers or closure you want, and you wrack your brain trying to figure out what went wrong. He was indifferent, he just couldn't commit, or he was immature.

Maybe *you* were the one who couldn't do it anymore, and you were just plain done. Perhaps you finally realized that you didn't really have that much in common after all, or the timing was bad, or he found someone else. Maybe you know exactly why you split up, and it makes you livid, depressed, or resentful. There are as many reasons as there are relationships. There's always the "I don't know what I want right now" explanation or the fear factor. Maybe you never had any good role models in your life of what a healthy love relationship or marriage looks like and it scares you to death. You're afraid to trust because you don't want to end up in an unhealthy, dysfunctional, or boring relationship—or one that falls apart again.

I was surprised when a man I'd been getting to know online for a few months sent me an e-mail to break things off by saying, "I was looking at my calendar for the next year and I'm going to be really busy." *Well then what were the past four let's-get-to-know-*

each-other-better months about? Was he really busy or was he afraid of a commitment? I guess I'll never know.

Sadly, you may never know the real reason why the person you once shared everything with will now tell you nothing.

Whether the final send-off came gradually or you were blindsided, endings are never easy. Katy and Will enjoyed a year of Saturday night indie films and Starbucks runs before Will shocked her one summer afternoon when he said he couldn't see himself marrying her. But he still wanted to "hang out," and Katy, not wanting to lose him entirely, continued to see Will for six more months—and in the process lost herself and her self-respect. Finally, she could no longer endure the emotional turmoil of longing and lack, hoping that one day he would come around. As she began to learn more about her true worth and value, she courageously broke it off entirely.

Unlike Katy's drawn-out breakup, Chaundra's ending was sudden. Darren exited as quickly as he entered her life. He was a "comet" dater—burn fast, burn bright, and burn out. From the day they met at her best friend's house, Darren called her every day (sometimes two or three times a day). After a few weeks of spending all of their free time together, he just stopped calling. No explanation. The next Saturday Chaundra saw Darren with another woman at a café and she was heartbroken.

RESPONDING TO "THE END"

Then there's your story. When you end a significant relationship, you may feel a hundred different emotions, from some snarly name-calling or a disillusioned, "I really thought this would go somewhere," to a despondent, "How am I going to get over him?" You're sad, angry, confused, hurt, depressed, and some days you just want to sob with your two new best friends, Ben and Jerry (and their ridiculously good frozen treats).

Everyone responds to loss and pain differently. For some of

us it takes longer to absorb the changes, adjust, and begin again. Whether you were together for a long time or a short time, you may have had a close, deep connection. Your personality, temperament, and background all make a difference in how you deal with emotional pain (or don't) and how long it takes to heal.

If you're the one breaking it off, you may be hurting someone you care about (or once cared about) and that can bring a host of emotions from guilt and shame to remorse and blame. No matter what the guy says—like the classic, "it's not you, it's me"—or how he says it (in person or by phone, fax, letter, e-mail, text, or other electronic media), your relationship has ended. Game over. You're not together anymore. Now what?

HOW DO YOU "JUST GET OVER IT"?

When it comes to breakups, everyone around you will most likely have an opinion, even your most well-intentioned friends. *Forget about it. There are other fish in the sea. I never liked him anyway. You're such a nice girl I'm sure you will find someone. Just get over it.* But how?

WITHOUT DEALING with your feelings, you wind up carrying your breakup baggage into the next relationship—and the next.

Maybe you don't want to "just get over it"; you want to curl up on the couch and cry, maybe even wallow, at least for a bit. Perhaps you don't know what to do, so you do nothing. Or worse, you find unhealthy ways of coping with your losses and attempt to numb out and anesthetize the pain of rejection with excessive eating, drinking, shopping, or partying, and you end up stuffed, sloshed, broke, and tired—and you still have a broken heart.

Then there's the Ice Woman approach, where you try not to feel anything at all because it just hurts too much to feel. Perhaps you rebound in a quick relationship with Mr. Right Now instead of holding out for Mr. Right. Without dealing with your feelings, you wind up carrying your breakup baggage into the next relationship—and the next.

How do you heal a broken heart? How do you get rid of the awful kicked-in-the-stomach feeling and become a person of resilience, courage, and joy? How do you leave . . . grieve . . . and learn to trust and love again? How do you begin again, especially when you just don't want to?

This book will cover those topics, but first let's get some perspective on endings and loss, some essential things to know on your heart-healing journey. Often we only see things from our own point of view, but God's perspective is larger. He sees the big picture of our lives; the past, present, and future, and He knows what is best for each of us.

ENDINGS ARE A PART OF LIFE

Endings are a part of life. In fact, much of life is about beginnings and endings, transitions and changes, losing and finding anew. You graduate from high school or college and start a job. You leave a job or ministry and launch into another one. Sometimes you move from one part of the country to another and begin all over again. Loss and gain, good and bad, life and death are all part of life, and life has its cycles.

For some, adjusting to the transition that conclusions bring is smooth, for others it's rocky and staggered. You will not stay in this ending phase of life forever; a new beginning will come. You may not know when or how, but it will. Just like the springtime comes every year, even after the hardest of winters.

If you pretend life is a storybook with only happy endings, it's not reality. Hard things happen. Sometimes we lose people or things we treasure. But it does not mean we are losers. I've heard that Chuck Swindoll says, "It's not what happens to you, it's how you respond to it that makes a difference."

You can choose to ignore your pain, or in the midst of your pain and darkness, you can look to the light of God's truth for hope, healing, and wholeness. Either way, it's your choice. How you handle endings, or don't, will determine how you move forward. The next few chapters will help you get there.

SOME ENDINGS ARE NECESSARY

It's probably the last thing you want to hear right now, but it's true: some endings are necessary. For example, if you were dating someone who treated you poorly, it's your gain, not your loss, that he's no longer in your life. Someone who is rude, obnoxious, or insulting is not a good choice of someone to bond with, much less spend the rest of your life with.

It's important to discern acceptable behavior—in any relationship. It is not acceptable to tolerate abuse (physical or emotional). Ever. Just as a green plant needs to be pruned in order to grow back healthier leaves, sometimes things need to be cut from our lives so we can heal and blossom. On the other hand, maybe this guy was amazing, but he was not the best choice, God's choice, for your marriage partner.

Endings come in life, but God will not leave you in a place of despair. In time, He will lead you on to beginning anew.

BREAKUPS HURT, BUT GOD HEALS

Have you ever seen a glass break and shatter across a floor? Hundreds of miniscule pieces scatter and leave a complete mess.

You wonder how it can ever be cleaned up or made right again.

Perhaps right now you feel like your heart is fractured like broken glass. Thankfully, the Master is the master at rebuilding brokenness. In His own way and His perfect timing, God restores the splintered fragments of a broken soul. In time you will be able to let go of the past and hold on to a faith that will lead you from sadness to joy, death to life, fear to faith, rejection to acceptance, and darkness to light.

There is more ahead for you—so much more. "No eye has seen, no ear has heard, no mind has conceived what God has prepared for those who love him" (1 Corinthians 2:9).

HEALING TAKES TIME—AND MORE

Don't be fooled into thinking time alone heals all wounds. It's the power of God that heals you, and He uses many avenues to bring about healing: time, the love and care of others, something you read in a book or hear in a sermon, your attitude and actions, and more.

God does His part, and we do our part. Our part begins by showing up and being faithful.

Of course, every relationship is unique, so your healing process—*how* you heal and the *amount of time* it takes—will be different for everyone.

In addition, people who have unhealed grief from the past (whether it's from childhood or previous relationships) will need more time to work through the heart-mending process. It may take your friend a few months to get over her breakup, and it may take you a year. God's methods and timing are unique to each circumstance. The main thing is: don't rush the healing process.

Whether this is your first big breakup or your fifteenth, letting go hurts. The amount of time you spent in the relationship, and how close you were both emotionally and physically all play a part in how long it takes to stop the heartache and move forward. It takes time to get used to being on your own again.

You may need a period of adjustment and emotional repair to steady your self after a tidal wave has rocked your "loveboat." Even a sailboat after a squall needs some time in dry dock to repair the hull and mend the sails. There will be new adventures ahead, but for now, it's heart-restoration time.

LIGHT OVERCOMES THE DARKNESS

When the power fails and the lights go out in your home, your natural reaction is to grab a flashlight so you can see. When difficult things happen, often people are tempted to hide or withdraw into the "darkness" of isolation, depression, or sin instead of reaching for their spiritual light source to illuminate the emotional darkness of their hearts. They don't want to deal with things they think will overwhelm them, or they simply don't have the resources to handle intense feelings.

Pain, anger, resentment, and betrayal are thorny issues. Rejection hurts, and the loss of love and affection can make us do crazy things sometimes. Without the light of God's truth to guide and heal us, we can gravitate toward dark habits and try to find our own temporary, unhealthy, or ineffective solutions to ease the pain.

A friend once told me, "Don't forget in the dark what you've learned in the light." In other words, remember God's good promises you learned in good times when the hard times come. Jesus said, "I have come into the world as a light, so that no one who believes in me should stay in darkness" (John 12:46).

Light always overcomes darkness. With the Light of the World, Jesus Christ, you can be encouraged, equipped, and empowered to journey through the stages of healing and find restoration and transformation.

You may not believe this right now, but the day will come when you don't think about him every day, and the mention of his name doesn't pierce your heart like a verbal arrow. You can drive past your special place and it no longer has a hold on you. It's just a place. You know who you are and what you want and it's okay. You know God loves you and He is with you. And that makes all the difference.

The sun sets, the heart breaks, but the light of God's brilliant and illuminating truth shines on. You come to realize that endings are a part of life, and so are new beginnings.

> THE SUN SETS, the heart breaks, but the light of God's brilliant and illuminating truth shines on.

And you learn that God heals brokenness and brings joy, hope, and healing. And one day everything really will be okay. Maybe not today, but someday. As the tears pour out you discover that everything happens for a reason, even when you don't understand or like it. Bleary-eyed, you look up and smile as it begins to settle in your heart that God really is in control; He knows what He's doing, He cares and is working all things together for the good whether the relationship door slammed shut or gently closed behind you.

A door closes, a window opens, and a fresh breeze blows into the stale mourning stillness that lingers in your heart. In the midst of your mess, God surprises you, and things begin to change.

A wise man named Solomon reminds us that, "There is a time for everything, and a season for every activity under heaven . . .

> a time to plant and a time to uproot, . . .
> a time to tear down and a time to build,
> a time to weep and a time to laugh,
> a time to mourn and a time to dance, . . .
> a time to embrace and a time to refrain,
> a time to search and a time to give up,
> a time to keep and a time to throw away,
> a time to tear and a time to mend."
> (Ecclesiastes 3:1–7)

What time is it in your life? The edge of evening is approaching, and it's time to get the comfort and support you need to begin the heart-healing process.

The rest of your life is waiting.

PRAYER

Lord, endings can be so hard. I wanted things to be different in my love life, yet here I am with a broken heart. Please help me, comfort me, and heal me. I need Your strength and power—Your love and light—to get through this dark time. Thank You for the assurance that You are with me every step of the way. Help me to trust You even when I do not understand. I know healing is a process and it takes time, so I need wisdom to wait on Your perfect timing for wholeness. I choose to follow Your healing path from darkness to light, from sadness to joy. Lead me to brighter days and a lighter heart. In Jesus' name, Amen.

LIGHT FOR THE JOURNEY

"Don't forget in the dark what you've learned in the light." One way to remember the light of God's truth is to surround yourself with it. Look up helpful Bible verses and write them on index cards or paper. Then post them in places you will see every day, like your bathroom mirror, dresser, or refrigerator (or carry them with you in your purse or wallet). When you read God's truth and connect with it, you will be changed. Power up with God's Word! Here are a few to get you started:

Let him who walks in the dark, who has no light, trust in the name of the Lord and rely on his God. (Isaiah 50:10)

And we know that in all things God works for the good of those who love him, who have been called according to his purpose. (Romans 8:28)

ILLUMINATION

1. Identify what stage you're in right now: Twilight (dealing with endings), Night (healing emotional pain), Dawn (awakening hope), or Day (moving forward).

2. Chuck Swindoll said, "It's not what happens to you, it's how you respond to it that makes a difference." What are some different ways you can choose to respond to your situation right now?

3. Losses need to be dealt with, not suppressed or ignored. What are some consequences that may occur if you try to "just get over it" and don't grieve your losses and process your emotional pain?

4. What is one thing you can do this week to change your perspective on your breakup?

The Edge of Evening: Getting Comfort and Support

2

May your unfailing love be my comfort.
—Psalm 119:76

It was strangely quiet on the evening flight across the Atlantic. I was returning to Denver after a mission trip and family visit in Europe. The flight attendants had finally ceased their endless bustling and dimmed the cabin lights.

I flipped on my overhead light and finished reading the last few pages of *The Sacred Romance* by John Eldredge. Tired, but inspired, I closed the book and closed my eyes. As I leaned back in my seat, a gentle phrase rolled over and over in my mind, "Rest in the comfort of My love." It was clear, but not audible, and strongly imprinted in my thoughts. *What was God trying to tell me?*

The phrase didn't seem to have any particular significance at the time, but the very next day—and for the next few years—I would come to rely heavily on those seven words and discover the true meaning of comfort.

The day after I arrived home I received an e-mail from the guy I'd been with for the past two years. Brent and I had been dating on and off for months, but this was the final shattering. He told me, via electronic media no less, that he "felt led" to date another woman, and this woman was a close friend of mine. I was stunned, shocked, frozen; I could not comprehend this new information. It simply didn't make sense. It felt like a double punch—rejection and betrayal—and I lost two really good friends as a result. Indeed, it was the final good-bye. Only I wasn't very good at good-bye.

After that dreadful e-mail I called Brent and he came over a few days later to talk about things in person. He stated his desire to continue our friendship and I looked at him like he was from another planet. As I stared at him quizzically, my thoughts were reeling: *Are kidding me?! I thought I was going to marry you; you start dating one of my friends, and you want me to be your pal? Not gonna happen!*

Days later, I began to rethink things and wondered if I was

wrong. Maybe I was supposed to be his friend; maybe that was the "Christian" thing to do. Perhaps I needed to put all my hurt and pain aside and just forgive and forget. I wanted to do the right thing but I was confused about what the right thing was. So I started to research forgiveness and tried to figure out what to do. I read lots of advice, and much of it was contradictory. It was exhausting. Meanwhile, my heart hurt miserably from his choices. There was so much I didn't know about getting over a breakup.

Everyone handles the demise of a relationship differently. While some women will flit from one relationship to another, hoping to fill the void of the one who just left, others will bury their pain in working long hours. We either eat too much to try and mask the pain, or we may not have much of an appetite at all. Some singles isolate themselves from people (and what they think will be further pain), or obsess about the relationship, replaying the past over and over again.

A few days after Brent's news to date someone else I began to feel the impact of what it meant. I would never share special moments with him again, or laugh over private jokes, or kiss him. He wouldn't be the one I'd turn to when I wanted to share my good news or to listen to me after a bad day at work. It was really over. The rejection, shock, loss, and sadness all came knocking at my door. In fact, they barged right in. It was beginning to sink in that this really was The End with him. The End. Roll the credits. But don't turn the lights up yet.

GET STABILITY

Breakups hurt because something has been wounded. But unlike most physical injuries, the pain is on the inside and you can't see it. You can, however, see the effects of being left or leaving, and often you feel it. No matter how long you've been together or who broke up with whom, the stress from the emotions of rejection, shock, anger, or betrayal can be felt in a variety of painful ways.

Much like a physical injury, an emotional wound needs care, comfort, and recovery time. In fact, Proverbs 13:12 states, "Hope deferred makes the heart sick, but a longing fulfilled is a tree of life." As much as you may want to, you cannot press a "Delete" button and make the pain go away.

In the initial stages—the first few days or weeks after a breakup—it's wise to protect your heart just as you would a broken arm. If you broke a bone, you wouldn't wait until you've called all your friends and asked them what to do. You'd immediately rush to the hospital and get a cast. Why? Because a cast protects the bone from further injury and it allows the healing and repairing process to begin.

> I'VE FOUND THAT being away from the other person completely was more healing in the long run.

Healing emotional pain from a relationship split begins when you stabilize the situation. It's often helpful to be away from the other person, to separate from the source of pain so you can prevent further injury and begin the healing process.

Like a cast, a heart boundary or emotional wall is for a time and for a purpose. Don't go back and keep having repeated post-breakup talks or interactions with the person who broke your heart. It can be extremely difficult, like withdrawal from a drug, to keep your hand off the phone, but it will be easier to heal in the end. Don't call or e-mail him just to see how he is, and don't drive by his house or office. You may be tempted to want to reach out to him and connect because that's what you're used to—it's comfortable and familiar—but your goal here is not connecting, it's disconnecting. It feels awful and lonely and different. But that's just part of the process.

If he is in the same singles group you attend, or if you have a lot of friends in common, it can be challenging to see him at events. But you can decide if you want to go or not. It's up to you. If you do see him, you can be polite and friendly, but don't engage in deep conversation or touching. That would be like having a broken arm in a cast and saying you just want to play a *little* bit of baseball. Not a whole game, mind you, just swing the bat a few times. Bad idea. It would cause extreme pain and impede your healing. It's not time to play ball right now, it is heart-mending time. And God knows the best time for you to get back in the game.

Of course, every situation is different. I'm not saying that you have to cut off all contact completely or forever. Some women I know have been able to be friends with people they've dated, but not right away. A time of separation is essential if you are ever going to have a platonic friendship in the future.

Breakups can be complicated, and you may need to have a few talks to get to the finale. But use wisdom and discretion. Hard as it can be, I've found that being away from the other person completely, at least initially, was more healing in the long run than the slow hanging-on-to-fragments-of-what's-left relationship death.

Pray about it and ask God how to best tie up the loose ends of your ending. A wise woman has self-respect and doesn't grovel; she knows when to walk away and to whom to run—into the arms of her First Love and Great Physician, Jesus. He is the One who "heals the brokenhearted and binds up their wounds" (Psalm 147:3).

Once a broken bone is set, it eventually heals. After the cast is removed, the doctor sends you to rehabilitation to strengthen the muscles, and if you do your exercises regularly, the arm becomes stronger and usable again. In fact, I've been told that where a broken bone is healed it grows back even stronger.

In the same way that a cast is for a time and a purpose, healing the emotional wreckage of your breakup is also for a season. You won't be in this painful place forever.

Though you may shun it initially, a covering of darkness (your "cast") can be a good thing—a time to hide, a time to heal. Refuge in the arms of the Lord Jesus is a safe place. In Psalm 91:1–4 we learn that:

> He who dwells in the shelter of the Most High will rest in the shadow of the Almighty.
> I will say of the Lord, "He is my refuge and my fortress, my God, in whom I trust."
> Surely he will save you from the fowler's snare and from the deadly pestilence.
> He will cover you with his feathers, and under his wings you will find refuge; his faithfulness will be your shield and rampart.

Psalm 32:7 echoes the protective hiding theme: "You are my hiding place; you will protect me from trouble and surround me with songs of deliverance."

Not only does He protect, God also shows us what to do next: "I will instruct you and teach you in the way you should go; I will counsel you and watch over you" (Psalm 32:8).

This sacred space with just Jesus and you can be a special time. Alicia Britt Chole in *Anonymous* talks about the hidden times in our lives. Whether we feel rejected, unnoticed, unworthy, or unseen, there are good purposes that can come from our time in the dark. Chole says,

There in the poorly lit crawl spaces of life (transitions, prolonged waiting, new additions to the family, preparatory education, relocation, unexplainable loss, extended illness, irresolvable conflict, and all else that tends to hide us) God builds within us a sturdy support system for our souls. If we do not respect his craftsmanship in unapplauded seasons, all that is visible in our lives will rest on a fragile foundation, and eventually—through the added weight the visible brings—we will experience collapse.[1]

Hide in Him. Rest in Him. The Lord is healing, repairing, and rebuilding your loss-weary heart. In doing so, He will also provide the comfort and support you need.

HEALING YOUR BROKEN HEART

Disappointment strikes everyone at some point in life, and right now you may be feeling disillusioned, depressed, or just downright angry. Whether your relationship ending was sudden or gradual, your life has a different pace now. It has more empty spaces. No morning e-mail or phone call to say hello, no special someone to do things with or listen to your stuff; you're on your own again.

When the intensity of an empty heart and empty arms comes over you, everything in you just wants to feel better. How will you find comfort? What brings you relief and reassurance? Here are some helpful ideas to help you get the solace and support you need—especially in the first few days and weeks.

LET YOURSELF CRY

Crying is a normal and healthy response to a sad situation. Perhaps you're a person who holds back tears. You may think that if you start crying, you will never stop. Let yourself cry. Just let it out. Even if you have to set a time limit, getting your feelings out in this way can be extremely healing.

In fact, tears bring cleansing and comfort. Author and speaker Jill Briscoe once said that "God gives us enough tears to keep our clay moist so He can mold us." We are the clay, He is the potter, and God is reshaping your life for a good and holy purpose.

I remember being on the edge of tears for the first few months after a long-term relationship breakup. Even going to church and listening to music were triggers for me. I could relate well to the writers of the Psalms, especially when one writer said, "My tears have been my food day and night" (Psalm 42:3).

And then I read something hopeful: "Weeping may endure for a night, but joy comes in the morning" (Psalm 30:5 NKJV). Joy *will* come again one day! Sorrow will not last forever. It may not be a twenty-four-hour cycle of a literal day, but one day you will not feel this pain. Let the tears flow, and eventually your sadness will turn to a smile.

In *A Message of Comfort & Hope*, Eugene Peterson says this about tears, "Joy comes because God knows how to wipe away tears, and, in his resurrection work, create the smile of a new life."[2]

FIND TRUE COMFORT

When false comforters leave you emotionally and physically stranded, that means it's time to say good-bye to imitations and hello to the real thing: the *true comfort* found in "the God of all comfort" (2 Corinthians 1:3). His love, His presence, and His Word are healing gifts. In fact, some of the first Scriptures Jesus read aloud in the temple were from the book of Isaiah and spoke of healing and comfort:

The Spirit of the Sovereign Lord is on me, because the Lord has anointed me to preach good news to the poor.

He has sent me to *bind up the brokenhearted*, to proclaim freedom for the captives and *release from darkness* for the prisoners, to proclaim the year of the Lord's favor and the day of vengeance of our God, to *comfort all who mourn*, and provide for those who grieve in Zion—to bestow on them a crown of beauty instead of ashes, the oil of gladness instead of mourning, and a garment of praise instead of a spirit of despair. They will be called oaks of righteousness, a planting of the Lord for the display of his splendor. (Isaiah 61:1–3, emphasis mine)

In the light of God's Word everything becomes clearer. One night, months after a traumatic breakup, I wondered what the Bible said about comfort so I got out my concordance and looked up *every single reference* to comfort in the entire book. There were about seventy verses listed; it was a long night! Some of them are listed at the end of this chapter.

It may be helpful and healing for you to look up Bible verses that are meaningful to you and write them in a notebook or on an index card. Then read them (even read them out loud in your prayer time) to seal up heart holes with His truth.

PERSEVERE IN PRAYER

Prayer is a vital key in your healing process. Why not start each day with prayer for wisdom, guidance, healing, and favor and end each day with a prayer of thanks and gratitude for all He's done for you that day (whether you enjoyed it or endured it)?

Picture yourself standing before the Lord with open hands, palms faced up. Ask God to help you to be okay with empty spaces in your life right now, and trust Him to fill your open hands with good things.

Worship also brings healing and comfort. More than just singing songs, worshiping God puts the focus on Him, not yourself, and can lead you to deeper levels of love in your relationship with God. Worship fills your heart and can take you to a place that is profoundly replenishing and good. It is a time to prepare your heart to hear what God has to say to you during the church service. As you enter into His presence, giving—your love, gratitude, adoration, and praise—you also end up receiving hope, healing, joy, and a fresh encounter with God.

When the Lord spoke to my heart on that airplane the night before an unexpected and difficult ending, and said, "Rest in the comfort of My love," I learned that His love never comes to an end; it is unfailing. Psalm 119:76 reads, "May your unfailing love be my comfort." I also discovered that not only does God's love comfort me, He also takes great delight in me! "The Lord your God is with you, he is mighty to save. He will take great delight in you, he will quiet you with his love, he will rejoice over you with singing" (Zephaniah 3:17).

As time went by, I found rest meant to "be still, and know that I am God" (Psalm 46:10). He would take care of me and heal my situation. I didn't have to make it all happen on my own. I could learn, as the New American Standard Bibles states, to "cease striving." Rest in the comfort of the One who loves you more than you know.

PUT HIS STUFF AWAY

It can be very helpful to put away reminders of the person who just dumped you. Sure you may want to linger over pictures of your once-beloved just a few more times. That can be healing for some people. But it's hard to move forward into your new future when mementos of your past are pulling you back.

If you're not ready to discard them, box up all the photos and treasured objects he gave you and put them in storage until the time is right to get rid of them. You may also want to think about deleting his phone number from your cell phone so you're not tempted to do some desperate dialing in a weak moment.

TALK WITH TRUSTED FRIENDS OR FAMILY MEMBERS

Albert Schweitzer once said, "At times our own light goes out and is rekindled by a spark from another person. Each of us has cause to think with deep gratitude of those who have lighted the flame within us." We need our friends to comfort and support us in our times of need.

Telling your story can help to ease your heart's pain and bring emotional healing. When someone listens, we feel validated. When someone empathizes, we feel comfort and relief. Talk to your close friends or family members about your breakup story, not to bash the guy or cause harm, but to get it out of you—to release it, so you can find freedom and healing.

However, be selective about how much you choose to tell and with whom you share. It can be natural to want to divulge all the details and tidbits of conversations you had with your ex-boyfriend. However, some friends, even close ones, may tell you that they just cannot listen to your story one more time. They'd rather hear the "sweetened condensed" version of what happened—short and sweet.

In time you learn who is safe to share with and who is not. Here is where a good Christian counselor can help. Don't be afraid to find a counselor who can be a vital bridge to help you get from where you are to where you want to be emotionally. Also, your friends may not know what you need, so tell them. "I could use a hug right now" or "I just need someone to listen for a while" or whatever brings you the most comfort and relief. Trusted friends will listen, pray for and with you, and be there when you need companionship.

WRITE IN A JOURNAL OR NOTEBOOK

Sue was twenty-six years old when her engagement ended. She was devastated, but her dad gave her some helpful advice.

He asked her, "Why would you want someone who doesn't want you?" and advised her to walk away. He also gave her a plaque which read, "No boy is worth crying over. And the one who is won't make you cry—Sarah Kane, Age 10." Sue keeps prayer journals and writes down her prayers.

As time passes, she reads over what she's written in the past and can see progress. Often, Sue said, she's reminded of how things that seemed so significant and catastrophic at the time didn't even matter to her later in life. In fact, it may have been a blessing she didn't receive what she *thought* she wanted years earlier.

Writing your thoughts and prayers in a journal or notebook can be very beneficial. When your feelings appear on a page (or even typed online), they are no longer swirling inside your head. You can vent your emotions, release your pain, and do so in the privacy of your personal journal.

Think about asking God these questions and writing down your answers: Lord, what do You want me to learn from this relationship that just ended? What are You teaching me during this healing time?

God has valuable life lessons in every season of our lives, even the dark times. But you don't have to be afraid of the dark. God may have hidden treasures for you during this healing season. "I will give you the *treasures of darkness*, riches stored in secret places, so that you may know that I am the Lord, the God of Israel, who summons you by name" (Isaiah 45:3, emphasis mine).

NURTURE YOUR SPIRIT

When your heart is hurting, it's helpful to take care of yourself and remember what makes you feel good. What would best nurture your soul, mind, and body right now? What brings you the most comfort when you need heart healing? Comfort comes in a variety of ways and uses some or all of our senses:

- the *touch* of a friend's hug, a therapeutic massage, or a warm comforter around you as you rest in an overstuffed chair by a roaring fire;
- the *sight* of the stunning beauty of God's creation (on vacation or right in your own backyard), or a redecorated apartment;
- the *smell* of fresh cut flowers filling your living room, or a new perfume;
- the *taste* of your favorite comfort foods (like creamy mashed potatoes or a hot caramel latte);
- the *sound* of relaxing music, the melody of a flowing river on a nature walk, or a phone call from a kind friend who is really good at cheering you up.

Here are some other ideas you may find relaxing and comforting:

- Take a warm bath or a hot shower.
- Listen to worship CDs.
- Get movement into your life. Go for walk, a bike ride, or head for the gym.
- Get enough sleep; rest is healing.
- Feed your spirit, not your stomach, by reading your Bible.
- Pray.
- Call a friend and get together.
- Go to a movie.
- Read a good book.
- Get a pet.
- Relax on the couch with lit candles nearby.
- Eat healthy food. Avoid too much sugar; it messes with your moods.
- Balance time with friends and time alone.

+ Beauty is healing. Get outdoors and into God's creation. Go to a neighborhood park or get out on the water with jet skis.
+ Visit an art museum.
+ Take a vacation. Even if you can only get away for a few hours, a change of scenery can be a retreat for your soul.

BE ENCOURAGED

This is a time of transition. You're going from couple to single, from a "we" to a "me." Change takes time and we all handle it differently, so be good to yourself in the process. When the winds of adversity and the winds of change blow across the landscape of your heart, you can know that strong breezes make you stronger.

> CREATE OR FIND beauty in life. . . nurture your spirit by finding what brings you comfort.

Interestingly, scientists in Arizona discovered this in the early 1990s. They created a controlled, indoor environment called Biosphere 2 which housed eight researchers for two years.

Here they studied the effects of air, water, and soil on the environment and learned, among other things, that trees need wind in order to grow strong and tall. Without wind and the resistance it provides, trees bent over and crept along the ground.[3] In the same way, instead of wilting, the winds from your difficulties and disappointments can make you stronger.

So now what? How do you get on with life? You get up, you get dressed, and you keep on going. But you are not alone. Armed with God's presence and His Word, you choose to believe what God says is true and you seek to live it—even when you don't feel like it.

Some days you will stumble and some days you will stand firm, but no matter what happens, you walk on, knowing that you are one step closer to brighter days ahead. You talk to your close friends or family members and get counseling, if needed. You write in your journal and spend time in prayer and worship. You create or find beauty in life and get enough rest, healthy food and movement. You don't isolate yourself, but nurture your spirit by finding what brings you comfort.

THE DOOR OF HOPE

There is a way that leads to heart healing and relationship recovery. It's the door of hope, and the way out is through. In Hosea 2:15 the Lord provided a "door of hope" for a troubled woman and restored her wayward life:

Therefore I am now going to allure her; I will lead her into the desert and speak tenderly to her. There I will give her back her vineyards, and will make the Valley of Achor a door of hope. There she will sing as in the days of her youth, as in the day she came up out of Egypt. (Hosea 2:14–15)

Achor means *trouble*. Could there really be a path that leads from trouble to hope? *The Message* Bible reads "I'll turn Heartbreak Valley into Acres of Hope." Are you willing to knock on the door of hope and ask Jesus to lead you in your healing journey? He invites you.

"Ask and it will be given to you; seek and you will find; knock and the door will be opened to you. For everyone who asks receives; he who seeks finds; and to him who knocks, the door will be opened" (Matthew 7:7–8). Ask. Seek. Knock.

The door is both an exit and an entrance. When you walk *through*, not around it or avoiding it, you continue your passage from the land of sadness and despair to a place of joy and restoration. Beyond the door is the lighted pathway to hope and wholeness.

PRAYER

Dear Lord, I am really hurting today. How could this happen? I simply do not understand. I am sad and angry and heart-broken. I give You my pain and cast my cares into the ocean of Your love and comfort. I choose to trust You, and remember that no matter what happens, You are faithful, kind, and good. Even when I do not see where the plot is going, You are still the author of my story. I need You, Lord. I need Your close pres-ence. Help me to rest in the comfort of Your love. Restore my shattered heart. In Jesus' name, Amen.

LIGHT FOR THE JOURNEY

God has valuable life lessons for us in every season of our lives, even the dark times. In your prayer time, ask God these questions and write down your answers: Lord, what do You want me to learn from this relationship that just ended? What are You teaching me during this healing time?

Here are some key verses on comfort from the Bible. Read them aloud to yourself or write them on an index card to post or carry with you.

I, even I, am he who comforts you. (Isaiah 51:12)

O my Comforter in sorrow, my heart is faint within me. (Jeremiah 8:18)

Blessed are those who mourn, for they will be comforted. (Matthew 5:4)

Praise be to the God and Father of our Lord Jesus Christ, the Father of compassion and the God of all comfort, who comforts us in all our troubles, so that we can comfort those in any trouble with the comfort we ourselves have received from God. (2 Corinthians 1:3-4)

ILLUMINATION

1. What hurts you most about the end of this relationship?

2. What do crying and tears mean to you? (e.g., Crying is not acceptable; I cry all the time; I am afraid to cry; I think I have a healthy attitude about shedding tears; etc.).

3. What types of things have you done in the past to find comfort or soothing from painful life experiences?

4. What are some new ways you can try to cope and find comfort now?

3 Nightfall:
Grieving Losses

How long must I wrestle with my thoughts
and every day have sorrow in my heart?
—Psalm 13:2

They say you never forget your first love. I will never forget my first big breakup. Saying good-bye to Matt wasn't like ending a high school romance or getting over a guy I'd dated a few times. He was the first of the big ones in the Breakup Big Leagues.

I met Matt in our church singles group a few years after I graduated from college. During our first date one fall, I discovered that Matt was interesting and easy to talk to. He was mature in his faith. He was kind. He listened attentively, and (gasp!) he asked me questions about *me*. Although I wasn't head over heels for him right away, I grew more in like with him as we dated over the next few months, and he continued to pursue me.

One evening during the following spring, we took a walk down a wooded path to enjoy the restful calm and the last lingering moments before sunset. I felt good about how things had been progressing with us, and as we walked hand in hand, I told him that I was committed to moving forward with him. He seemed overjoyed, and we strolled back content and happy.

The next day he ended our relationship.

What? Why? I was stunned. Matt told me that once I decided I was "all in," he had to back out because *he* wasn't ready to make a commitment—he was still pining over the woman who'd previously dumped him, and had been throughout our entire relationship. He still believed that she was "The One" for him (despite knowing she was dating someone else now) and he couldn't be with me if there was still some chance he could have her.

Like a tornado on the Kansas prairie, emotions swirled wildly around in my head: I was bewildered, confused, hurt, mad, and sad. I forgot to eat at times, and lost a lot of weight. I couldn't sleep well and cried often. Since it was my first big breakup, I didn't know what to do to make the pain go away, or how to process the hurt in healthy ways.

Even after my second Big League breakup a few years later, I was gloomy for months. Seeing someone that resembled Chad, or smelling his cologne on a passing stranger would send my emotions reeling. I pined for this guy for well over a year, hoping he would change his mind and come back. Instead, he married, divorced, and was now living with a woman somewhere west of the Rockies. Clearly his faith had gone down a different path, and I could only see in hindsight that he was not right for me and that God was protecting me from so much pain.

So much pain.

HEALING IS A JOURNEY

Healing a broken heart is a journey—from sadness to joy, anger to peace, rejection to acceptance, and brokenness to a greater level of wholeness—and the road to recovery is different for everyone. That's because loss is different for everyone. Indeed, loss is personal. *How* you get over someone you once liked or loved and *how long* it takes will vary.

It's important to note that the healing takes place *in the journey*, not at the destination. The lessons you learn along the way and the choices you make can change and transform the landscape of your heart. But remember: it's a process, and healing takes time. You don't immediately leave The Land of Loss and Pain and arrive in The Land of Joy and Peace all at once. Heart healing comes one step at a time, one choice at a time, and one day at a time.

Finally, after my third Big League breakup I went to see a Christian counselor. She gave me some helpful insights and opened my eyes to ways that I could process the pain. One day after my counselor and I had prayed together, I went home and wrote this story about my last breakup—where I'd been and where I was headed, to a better place of healing and hope. As you read it, think about your own breakup and how it is a journey *from* a place of pain and endings *to* a place of joy and new beginnings. You're going somewhere, you are not alone, and you don't have to stay in this place of heartache forever. If you choose to embark on your own healing journey—to grieve your losses and process your emotional pain—you will never be the same again.

THE DESERT STORY

It was no ordinary rainy day; it was a downpour. I was driving alone in an unfamiliar place while heavy rain beat on the windshield of my car. The wiper blades could not keep up with the waterfall dropping from the sky and into my life.

I had been feeling distressed and lost after a relationship breakup, but I didn't know how to get out of the storm and back into the sunshine. I needed direction and a way out of my pain. The ominous gray clouds gave no sign of budging and the rain pounded steadily. I could no longer see the road in front of me; I had to pull over.

As I approached the side of the road, a police officer appeared, standing in the rain. I rolled down my window and asked, "How do I get out of this storm?" He leaned down to my level and replied, "Keep on going," and pointed straight ahead.

Uncertain, I asked, "Are you sure? Are you sure that is the way?" He smiled and said, "Yes, keep on going. That is the way." I persisted. I needed to know with certainty that I was heading in the right direction. "Are you *sure?*" I asked again. Still smiling, he patiently repeated, "Yes, I have been that way many times. That is the way."

He seemed to know what he was talking about. I rolled up my window and drove on, straight ahead through the storm. If *he* had traveled this road already then I knew that I would eventually leave this gloomy place and find sunshine again. I drove on.

Suddenly, it stopped raining. I had been driving in it so long that the abrupt ending startled me. I pulled my car to the side of the road and got out. I was thrilled to see the clear blue sky again!

Indeed the rain had ended, but I was not prepared for the view in front of me. I was up high on a plateau and could see for miles ahead of me a vast desert with a winding road. It wasn't a sandy desert with dunes like the Sahara; it was rocky, barren, and empty. A twisting road meandered from where I was standing, through the desert, and led to a land in the distance with lush green trees, mountains, and lakes. I was surprised that I could see that far ahead as I pondered the contrast of the hot, barren desert and the cool mountain scene beyond.

There was a distinct dividing line between where the desert ended and the flourishing place began. It must be my Promised Land, my place of no pain and better days. But in order to get there, it seemed, I had to go through this desolate place first.

I was confused and a bit disappointed. I had just driven through a terrible storm and I was worn out. Now I had to trek through a desert? I just wasn't up to it. I closed my eyes and prayed, "Lord, I don't want to go through a desert. I just got out of a storm."

"I will be with you.'"

"But it will be hot," I countered.

"I will be your fan."

I had to make a decision—go through the desert in order to get to my Promised Land or go back to the storm. I chose to walk on. It was unfamiliar territory, and I had many questions about the road ahead. With all the winding switchbacks, I wouldn't be able to see around the bend, and there were many bends. How would I survive? All I knew of the desert was that it was blazing hot in the daytime and cold at night. I would need relief and protection.

The Lord said, *"Abide."*

Abide? What did that mean? Walk on, but with Him. He would be my hiding place, my oasis in the desert. He would guide and provide. I would not only survive, but thrive as I resided with Him and trusted—in a storm, in a desert, or anywhere.

This story was a picture of what God was doing in my life to get me from a stormy relationship breakup to a healing place of joy, peace, and freedom: my Promised Land. This verdant place of abundance did not represent heaven, where all pain goes away forever and we experience complete and total wholeness. Instead, this was the John 10:10 life that Jesus promised us here on earth when He said, "I have come that they may have life, and have it to the full."

A WAY OUT

You may have heard about some other people who had to go through a desert experience to get to a better place. The Old Testament book of Exodus tells the story of their "way out" of oppression and misery and into a better place.

For 430 years the Israelites lived as foreigners in Egypt, many of those years under forced slavery. Then God called Moses to rescue them, but the road to freedom was fraught with obstacles. Moses was afraid and felt unqualified for the job, but God reminded him, "I will be with you" (Exodus 3:12).

At first, the Egyptian king, Pharaoh, refused to let the people leave his country. But after many plagues and deaths he relented. Finally the exit began, and more than half a million people were mobilized to quickly get out of town.

God led the Israelite people in a wilderness way, but He went ahead and provided light at night and a cloud by day so they could move forward (Exodus 13:21–22).

Many things happened on that journey from bondage to a better land, but because of their disobedience and wandering hearts, their eleven-day trip took forty years.

After Moses died, his aide, Joshua, took over as the leader. He listened to God and courageously led the Israelites across the Jordan River, through many battles and victories, and finally got the job done—they entered the Promised Land!

In his final days, Joshua reminded the people about how God always took care of them and kept His promises. "You know with all your heart and soul that not one of all the good promises the Lord your God gave you has failed. Every promise has been fulfilled; not one has failed" (Joshua 23:14).

THE IMPORTANCE OF GRIEVING LOSSES

As God kept His promises with Moses and Joshua, He will keep His promises to you. He will be *with you*. The Lord knows you are hurting, and you don't have to go through this time of pain alone. He will lead, guide, and provide light for every step in your heart-healing journey. You just have to trust Him.

One of the most essential lessons I learned in my season of desert darkness was the importance of grieving losses—going *through*, not around the pain. It was a pivotal point in getting to freedom and joy.

I remember standing in a local bookstore reading an endorsement on the back of *The Grief Recovery Handbook* by John W. James and Russell Friedman. It was one of those "aha" moments when your heart says, "That's what I need!" A professor who used the book for his college classes, Bernard McGrane, PhD, professor of sociology at Chapman University said, "I believe that unresolved grief is the major underlying issue in most people's lives."[1]

Unresolved grief? I knew I was sad and hurt from my last breakup. But it had never occurred to me that I had "grief" and it had to be resolved. Wasn't grieving for getting over a death?

In the ensuing months, I came to learn that grieving was for all sorts of losses. It gave me a name for the permeating sadness I'd been feeling for months.

Why do people avoid processing emotional pain, especially when emotions are strong? For one thing, as Mr. Griffen said to Annie in the movie *We Are Marshall*, "Grief is messy." Mascara runs down your face when you cry, your eyes get puffy, and your nose gets red. Your emotions fluctuate like the highs, lows, and unexpected turns of a roller-coaster ride. It's not pretty. But then again, neither is a rainstorm in springtime when the roads flood and the mud slides. But grieving, like spring—the shoulder between the dead of winter and the glory of summer—lasts only for a season.

> I CAME TO LEARN
> that grieving was
> for all sorts of losses.

Maybe you've seen people who try to hide their pain. They put on a pretend smile when inside they are dying emotionally. Like a duck gliding along the surface of a pond, they seem calm and unruffled, while underneath they're paddling like mad just to stay afloat.

If you are going through a bad breakup and want to get over it, it's important to know what grief is, why it's important to process it, and how to go through it.

WHAT IS GRIEF?

While most people associate grief with physical death, James and Friedman give us a much broader definition: "Grief is the normal and natural reaction to loss of any kind."[2] Grieving is not just okay, it's necessary. "The problem," they continue, "is that we have all been socialized to believe that these feelings are abnormal and unnatural."[3]

The truth is, people who have experienced a traumatic event or loss, like a relationship breakup, may react in similar ways to someone dealing with a death. And that is completely normal. While everyone processes grief differently, there are some often-recognized patterns or stages of grief.

STAGES OF GRIEF

Shock—You may feel immobilized, numb, or frozen when you initially hear your relationship is ending.

Denial—As a way of coping, you may tell yourself, "This is not happening," because you are not yet able to accept the reality of the events around you.

Anger—You may think, "It's not fair!" or "Why is this happening?" as you experience anger, guilt, or both emotions. If you were blindsided by the breakup and the loss was unexpected, your feelings may be intense.

Bargaining—You want to make a deal with God and try to get the other person back into your life. You may plead, "I'll pray more, I promise," or ask "If I (fill in the blank), will You let us stay together?" as you bargain for another chance.

Depression—In this stage, you may feel a range of sadness, from misery to excruciating pain. Some people even have problems getting out of bed because they lack purpose and find no reason to move into a new day.

Acceptance—Finally, you come to a place where you accept the loss. It happened. You may not like it or agree with it, but you learn to live with things as they are now and you find other ways to fill your life. Getting to acceptance can take a long time—months or even years. More on this topic is covered in chapter 6 which deals with the power of forgiveness.

Working through the stages is not a linear process. Like a

curvy mountain road with switchbacks, the journey of dealing with emotional pain is not a straight line. There is no set schedule or timetable; God works differently in each of our lives. Yet despite the twists, turns, and emotional weaving through the steps, dealing with the pain (not avoiding it) helps you to eventually get through it.

WHY DEAL WITH BREAKUP GRIEF?

Once you are aware of the stages, you can choose what you will do next. Will you deal with your breakup grief or stay stuck in your isolation and pain? Emotional pain won't just go away if you ignore it. In fact, it is widely known that holding back emotions or not dealing with them can lead to increased stress and even physical illness.

For example, "Stress can lead to exhaustion, weakness, headaches, indigestion, shortness of breath, loss of appetite, and inability to sleep."[4] The effects of loss come in a variety of ways, like "shock, numbness, denial, intense crying . . . a prolonged period of sorrow, restlessness, apathy, memories of the past, loneliness, and sleep disturbances."[5]

Whether you respond initially to a breakup with shock, numbness, or denial, eventually the full impact of the loss will surface. But you can eventually come to terms with it and find peace if you take action to deal with your pain.

GETTING UNSTUCK

A loss of significance—a big loss—can get stuck in your heart if it is not processed. When your self-esteem falters, and you feel like it's always midnight, the pain can pile up like emotional garbage. Grief left unattended, like refusing to deal with the hurt or holding your feelings inside, clogs the drain, blocking your emotions as well as your movement forward into healing and wholeness.

Stuck pain can also lead to unwanted behavior. You're constantly sad or bitter and it keeps you at arm's length from other people, so you feel alone. You don't feel like yourself, so you end up saying or doing things you don't really mean—like blaming others or lashing out in unwarranted anger—and hurting others.

It's been said that if you don't grieve well, you grieve all the time. While you may put on a good front for friends and coworkers, inside the lingering sadness remains. On the other hand, when you express your grief and deal with it, you can become emotionally stronger and healthier. That's why it's so important to grieve losses—to unblock your frozen heart so you can feel better, find joy, and live a life of emotional freedom, serenity, and love.

It's time to "drain the pain," and express your grief so you can move forward.

HOW TO EXPRESS YOUR GRIEF

Everyone heals in their own way and their own timing because love and loss is unique for each person. Here are some ideas on how to process your pain and release your sadness through grieving.

Acknowledge your loss. Getting through this season of grief and sadness begins by acknowledging that a loss has happened. Whether you left, he left, or it was a mutual agreement, something that was there is now gone.

Ask for help. Pray and ask the Holy Spirit to help you do what you cannot do on your own. With His power, emotions expressed will begin the flow, unclogging your blocked heart. In time you will get unstuck and move from the darkness of loss and pain into the sunlight of restoration and wholeness. After all, "The Lord upholds all those who fall and lifts up all who are bowed down" (Psalm 145:14).

Also, ask for help from a close friend or family member who will listen as you share your breakup story. When someone listens to your heart, hears your pain, and witnesses your sorrow, it can be life-changing.

I'll never forget how my good friend Andy helped release a deeper level of sadness in me from a devastating breakup. One night after Bible study, we were talking about the guy who'd hurt me. Soon I was a bucket of tears, but my caring friend enveloped me in a comforting hug and held me while I cried. He prayed over me and comforted me. In the arms of a man I knew and trusted I felt sad but safe, and then experienced remarkable relief. His act of genuine brotherly love was a turning point for me that night as the last remnants of grief fell away.

Let yourself be sad. "Sorrow is entirely underrated," writes Tim Baker in his book *Broken*.[6] "Sometimes," he continues, "we feel that crying is showing weakness and that real Christians, if they're truly saved, would never feel sorrow or cry."[7] Nothing could be further from the truth. Tears are a cleansing emotional release from a wellspring deep inside of us that need to get out. Tears are part of unblocking our inner stuckness and pain. "It is as if we have to cry so the pain has somewhere to go, and that somewhere is out of us," says Baker.[8]

Remember that even Jesus wept when He arrived on the scene where His dear friend Lazarus had been buried (John 11:35). He cried even though He knew Lazarus would rise again in mere moments! If Jesus grieved a loss which would soon be reversed, certainly we can give ourselves permission to grieve our losses as well.

Whether you cry alone or in the company of a trusted friend, the Lord knows and cares about your heartaches: "You keep track of all my sorrows. You have collected all my tears in your bottle. You have recorded each one in your book" (Psalm 56:8 NLT).

What do you need to release today? Will you release the pain, release control, release your need to be right, release the other person from what he or she did to you—or didn't?

> # GOD REDEEMS loss
> and pain and heals
> the heart to love again.

Recognize what you've lost and what remains. It can be helpful to make a list of your losses. Beyond losing a significant love relationship, you may have also lost companionship and friendship, affection, hopes and dreams for the future, trust, control, self-respect, or self-esteem.

While working though loss can be devastatingly difficult, it's comforting to know that God redeems loss and pain and heals the heart to love again. The word "redeem" means "to trade in, exchange, or transfer." God excels at converting heartache to healing, and redeeming things that have been tossed away into something worthy and wonderful.

Think about what remains and make a list of those things, too. Whatever your list includes, know that God's love goes on. He cares, He comforts, and He is near to those who hurt. "The Lord is close to the brokenhearted and saves those who are crushed in spirit" (Psalm 34:18).

Dig into God's Word. The Psalms offer a great example of being honest with God about pain, but also acknowledging that He is still faithful. Psalmists often cried out to God with disappointment, sadness, longings, and doubt. And yet, they would soon remember God's goodness in bringing them through their trials. The psalmist wasn't afraid to express how he really felt, yet found, in the "but God" moments, a transition from tears to trust, from sorrow to celebration, or from heartbreak to hope.

In Psalm 13:2, for instance, David laments, "How long must I wrestle with my thoughts and every day have sorrow in my heart? How long will my enemy triumph over me?" Then later says, "*But* I trust in your unfailing love; my heart rejoices in your salvation. I will sing to the Lord, for he has been good to me" (Psalm 13:5–6, emphasis mine).

Psalm 71 reveals the anguish of someone in dire need, "Be not far from me, O God; come quickly, O my God, to help me" (Psalm 71:12). The writer then finds hope and praises God, "*But* as for me, I will always have hope; I will praise you more and more" (v. 14, emphasis mine).

Pray. The most important thing you can do to heal your broken heart is to pray. It doesn't have to include elaborate words; it can be simple and heartfelt—as if you were talking to a friend, because indeed you are. Prayer changes things—and it changes us. Whether you pray alone, with friends, or with a prayer partner, talking and listening to God in a holy dialogue is essential to healing.

No matter what your circumstances, prayer is powerful. In Psalm 4:1, David said, "Answer me when I call to you, O my righteous God. Give me relief from my distress; be merciful to me and hear my prayer." We know that God hears our prayers and answers with what is best—in His way and in His time.

Later, when David was afraid because he was being chased by King Saul who wanted to kill him, he prayed intensely and often. When God answered his prayers, he was a happy man! "I sought the Lord, and he answered me; he delivered me from all my fears"

(Psalm 34:4). Not only was he joyful, he overcame and went on to extol many of God's good qualities in the rest of the verse.

Grieving losses is difficult, sometimes gut-wrenchingly hard, but you can get through it. As night falls and darkness settles in your heart-healing journey, you may feel afraid to walk on. But take heart. Grieving, like nighttime, will not last forever. Remember, you're just passing through on your way to better days. Much better days.

Prayer by prayer and moment by moment, healing comes. With the light of Christ to illuminate the way, things begin to change, or you change, or both. You start to reorient your life around other events, places, or people, and in time you return to a happier version of yourself with less sadness and more joy.

Keep on. For as you process and release the heartaches of today, you come closer to the goodness, freedom, and hope of tomorrow.

PRAYER

Dear Lord, I feel miserable. My heart is broken and I want to get beyond this pain. Will You help me to get unstuck and move forward into joy? I need Your healing power and love to get me through. Lord, I choose to give You my pain and losses. I leave all of them at the foot of Your throne and release them. I cast my cares. Be near me in this dark season. Through this loss, I am thankful for what remains—my health, my friends and family, and mostly for You. Thank You for Your care, comfort, and close presence. I know that You are with me every step of the way. Lead me, moment by moment, from sadness to joy. In Jesus' name, Amen.

LIGHT FOR THE JOURNEY

Make a list of what you've lost because of this breakup. Your "Things I've Lost" list may include people and feelings, not just things. For example, "I've lost love, affection, someone to do things with, the dream of marrying this person," etc.

Make a list of what remains. Your "Things That Remain" list could include positive things about you or things you are thankful for. For example, "What remains for me are: God (who never leaves me), my really good friends, my supportive family, hope," etc.

ILLUMINATION

1. What are some of the effects of a loss?

2. How do you generally handle sadness? Are you able to cry or do you hold your feelings inside?

3. What does it mean to grieve losses?

4. What is your response to this quote, "God redeems loss and pain and heals the heart to love again"? What does the word "redeem" mean to you in healing your breakup?

Part 2: Night

4 The Midnight Hour: Healing Emotional Pain

In choosing to face the night,
I took my first steps toward the sunrise.
—Gerald Sittser

The start of a new relationship is often bliss. Robert Browning must have been in love when the poet penned, "God's in his heaven—all's right with the world."

Then Cloud Nine bursts and suddenly, you're left to sort through a host of unruly emotions. What do you do with them? Or should you do anything with them?

Emotions are normal. We all have them, but we may express them differently. Or, we don't express them at all. After something as difficult as breaking up with someone you liked or loved, many people feel sad, anxious, or angry. But the emotion itself isn't as important as *what you do with it*. For instance, instead of talking it out or praying it out to release your feelings, you may—for whatever reasons—hold emotions inside or avoid feelings all together.

Though you may not want to face how you're feeling, dealing with emotions is essential to your emotional, physical, and spiritual health. Left untreated or unexpressed, breakup pain can prevent you from moving forward or wreak havoc in your love life. You may sabotage a perfectly good relationship because of your own commitment fears. Or, you may withhold affection and trust because others have wounded you deeply.

It may feel like one of the hardest, darkest times in your life right now—the blackest midnight—but the good news is that you can get rid of emotional pain. Your relationship may be over, but your life isn't. It's time to get some *life* back into your life!

By *identifying, expressing,* and *releasing* emotions, you can move through the process to get rid of the heartache and be better prepared for the kind of relationship you truly desire. In time, night will give way to a brand-new day, your new beginning.

Chloe had been walking in a cloud of depression for weeks. Even the daylight felt dim to her. After her breakup with Jared, she felt like she was in a fog of sadness. But what she didn't know was that hidden beneath her melancholy mood was a boatload of anger.

When she finally talked with a Christian counselor, she learned that instead of expressing her anger, Chloe was turning it inward toward herself and it was leading to her depression.

As a child, Chloe had observed other family members getting extremely out of control with their tempers—it was actually rage, but she didn't know that then. So she decided she would *never* get angry because she didn't want to be like them. She stuffed it all inside and thought she was doing the right thing.

Once she identified the emotion of anger and learned that it encompassed a range of emotions (from a mere annoyance to anger to full-blown rage), Chloe could acknowledge that emotion and learn to express it in healthy ways.

A social worker friend of mine uses tools like pictures or photographs of people that display various emotions to help clients identify and then work through their feelings. Journaling can also be helpful. As you write about what's happening in your life because of the breakup, certain themes may emerge. Even if they don't, you can get closer to acknowledging how you feel and what could be causing you to feel that way by writing in a notebook or journal: "I feel _____ when _____ happens." For example, I feel hurt when he lies to me. Or, I feel deceived because she went out with him behind my back.

HOW TO DEAL WITH ANGER

Taliesha was mad. After dating her boyfriend Marcus for *three years*, she had asked him if he could ever see them marrying each other. "I don't know," Marcus had replied, "I feel like I don't really know you," and refused to discuss it further. He didn't want to share his feelings, as usual, and it appeared he didn't want to share his life with her either. Taliesha and Marcus broke up shortly after that revealing conversation.

We all get angry once in a while and that's normal. But when we ignore it, hide it, or express anger destructively, then it's a problem. Fully God and fully man, even Jesus felt and expressed righteous anger during His time on earth (John 2:13–17).

It's important to understand that anger is a secondary emotion. In other words, before we feel angry, we first feel a different, primary emotion, such as hurt, fear, or frustration. In order to really deal with our anger, we need to address what first caused it. Think about it for a moment. Right before you became angry, what did you feel?

Anger is a signal that something is not right, and how you choose to handle that emotion makes all the difference. While our hearts may scream that we've been wronged and we yearn for justice, we need to be guided by God's Word, not our feelings. Ephesians 4:26–27 reads, "'In your anger do not sin': Do not let the sun go down while you are still angry, and do not give the devil a foothold." Don't give in to rage, hostility, violence, cruelty, or physical or verbal abuse.

Here are some other key verses that can help keep anger in check:

Get rid of all bitterness, rage and anger, brawling and slander, along with every form of malice. Be kind and compassionate to one another, forgiving each other, just as in Christ God forgave you. (Ephesians 4:31–32)

My dear brothers, take note of this: Everyone should be quick to listen, slow to speak and slow to become angry, for man's anger does not bring about the righteous life that God desires. (James 1:19–20)

Watch your tongue and keep your mouth shut, and you will stay out of trouble. (Proverbs 21:23 NLT)

Here are some practical things you can do to manage your anger wisely:

Write an anger letter expressing to God your feelings about what happened during your breakup and/or since then. It can even include things that happened during the time you dated, if needed. "Pour out your hearts to him, for God is our refuge" (Psalm 62:8).

Or, you could write a different kind of anger letter. This exercise helps you to get the release you need, but you never mail the letter. Picture the person who broke up with you sitting across the table from you as you write. If you could say anything you wanted to him right now, what would you say? If you could say anything to him in a Christlike way, what would you say?

No one else will ever see what you write in either letter, so you can feel safe to express yourself, vent, and be free of the tangled emotions inside of you. When you're done, you can choose to burn or shred your letter if you'd like, but never (never!) mail it.

Write an anger action plan. In the midst of a heated conversation, sometimes you may need to leave so you (or the other person) can cool off and address your issues later. When you need to think through why you're irritated, this exercise can be helpful. Make a list of what happened, if you need to respond (you may not), how it makes you feel, and some potential ways you can respond. Then, after you've reviewed your options you can choose what to do. It will be helpful to pray before you begin. For example:

What happened? Tony constantly cuts me off before I can finish a sentence.

Do I need to respond? Yes, I feel like I need to stand up for myself.

How does this make me feel? I feel angry when Tony doesn't let me finish what I'm saying. I feel like he thinks what he has to say is more important than what I want to say. I feel diminished and unimportant.

How can I respond? When Tony cuts in when I'm talking, I could say, "Could I please finish my sentence?" or "I wasn't done yet." Or, I could spend less time with Tony. Or . . . ?

There are other ways to manage your anger, too. Some people find it helpful to punch pillows, talk to a trusted friend, pull out the Bible and read, journal their thoughts, go work out, or get outside for a long walk or bike ride. A good hearty laugh or getting some humor into your life can advance your heart toward joy again. Find activities that relieve stress for you—without hurting others.

HOW TO HANDLE REJECTION

No matter how hard someone tries to carefully choose their words as they are giving you the relationship send-off, rejection hurts. Whether you were together two weeks or two years, being rejected can leave you feeling unwanted, insecure, or "less than." Now you're excluded from his life, and maybe from his friends, mutual friends, or his family. Somehow it doesn't seem right that you lose this whole other community because you two are no longer together.

When you feel rejected, it's important to remember that there's "what happened" and "what you tell yourself" about what happened. Often, he is not rejecting you as a person, but making a choice on who is the best fit for him (just as you make a choice on who is the best fit for you). In addition, this man may have his own issues to deal with, and when he says, "It's not you, it's me," it may really be about his shortcomings.

It's important to know that not being chosen doesn't mean you're not acceptable. You are still worthy and wonderful whether the other person realizes it or not. You may not feel very wonderful right now, but don't let what someone else thinks erode your sense of self. Chapter 9 is an excellent resource on restoring confidence and self-esteem.

We all have a need for acceptance, belonging, and connection. But people who have experienced rejection or abandonment in their past (or who've been raised in an unpredictable or unstable environment) may feel a deeper reaction to rejection. They may have a harder time letting go of a romantic relationship.

> KEEP REMINDING yourself of the truth, because *truth combats lies like light overcomes darkness.*

When the past is bursting into your present, ask yourself, "What is it in my past that I need to deal with?" It may be something obvious or something that will come out as you think and pray about it. Your past doesn't have to overwhelm you, and you can find healing. Perhaps your breakup can be a springboard to propel you to make some life changes or get Christian counseling to deal with what happened long ago.

No matter who initiated the breakup, you will always be significant and important in the eyes of the One who loves you most. Keep reminding yourself of the truth, know it and live it, because *truth combats lies like light overcomes darkness.* The truth is, you matter to God, and He has unending love for you. You are accepted—totally and unconditionally. You are the apple of His eye. He chose you. You are enough, and *you are worth being loved well.* Truly, your love life matters to God. He is still in control, and He is leading you on a path to good purposes.

Jesus knows well the sting of rejection, and He can relate to your pain. Isaiah 53:3 tells us, "He was despised and rejected by men, a man of sorrows, and familiar with suffering. Like one from whom men hide their faces he was despised, and we esteemed him not." His worth and value weren't appreciated by some of the very people He came to save. Yet Jesus solidly knew who He was and where He was headed, and He changed the world forever. If we, too, can solidly grasp who we really are and embrace the reality of who God is, then we can become not only overcomers, but life-changers as well.

TIPS ON HANDLING FEAR

Rejection and fear go hand in hand. *What if I'm making a mistake by leaving him? What if no one ever loves me again? What if I'm too old, too fat, too thin, too boring, too undereducated, or too whatever? What if I never get married and have kids? What if . . . ?*

Fears can be crippling, paralyzing you from moving forward and taking risks in the future. It's important to know that while some fears are founded, others are irrational and will never come to pass. Whether your fear is rational or irrational, it needs to be confronted so you can find relief and victory.

You may have heard the saying "feel the fear and do it anyway." Sometimes we need to push past how we feel in order to do the right thing, or get where we need to be in life. With the power of the Holy Spirit, courage replaces fear as we take a step of faith and grow stronger in ways we never could have imagined.

The disciple named Peter did a very courageous thing when he decided to trust Jesus and defy gravity by walking on water. In Matthew 14:22–33 you can read the account of Peter and other disciples who were in a boat some distance from the shore when they saw Jesus walking on the lake. They thought it was a ghost and they were terrified.

Then Jesus told them not to be afraid and revealed to them it was Him. Peter replied to Jesus saying, "Tell me to come to you on the water." And Jesus said, "Come."

Interestingly, Peter got out of the boat and walked on the water toward Jesus. But when he looked around and saw the wind, he became afraid and began to sink into the lake. As he began to descend he cried out, "Lord, save me!"

Immediately Jesus reached out His hand to Peter and lifted him up, asking Peter why he doubted. When the two of them climbed into the boat, the wind died down and the disciples (who were most likely in awe) recognized that He was indeed God and worshiped Him.

When Peter's eyes were on Jesus he stood firm; but when his eyes were on his circumstances he sank. He learned a huge lesson in trust that day.

The Lord wants you to be free from fear, worry, and obsessive reasoning. He wants you to trust Him. When you do, the rewards are great. Instead of fear, doubt, and panic, there is freedom, peace, and joy.

Second Timothy 1:7 reminds us that God has not given us a spirit of fear but of power, and in 1 John 4:18 we learn that "there is no fear in love." Here are some other verses to reflect on as you conquer your fears:

The Lord is my light and my salvation—whom shall I fear? The Lord is the stronghold of my life—of whom shall I be afraid? (Psalm 27:1)

In God I trust; I will not be afraid. What can man do to me? (Psalm 56:11)

When I am afraid, I will trust in you. (Psalm 56:3)

So do not fear, for I am with you; do not be dismayed, for I am your God. I will strengthen you and help you; I will uphold you with my righteous right hand. (Isaiah 41:10)

DEALING WITH SHAME AND BLAME

Vanessa could not believe she went so far physically with Carlos while they were dating. She took pride in her values and was always able to keep boundaries with men, at least until he came along. But Vanessa was certain that Carlos would one day be her husband, and somehow it didn't seem so wrong if they were going to be married "someday." But they never got married. Carlos left her and started dating another girl and Vanessa was devastated. Unresolved shame gnawed at her soul.

Maybe you feel embarrassed because of things you said or did during your breakup. Or perhaps he dishonored you in how he treated you while you were dating and you feel humiliated or disgraced.

Guilt often leads to shame, but it's important to distinguish the two emotions. Simply put, shame is living in the darkness and grace is living in the light. Guilt says, "I did something wrong." Shame says, "Something is wrong with me." When a person feels shame, you feel like something is wrong with you whether it's true or not. You may feel inadequate, incompetent, or simply not good enough. Another person's hurtful words can make you feel belittled or unworthy. Because of what another person does to us, or what we tell ourselves, we can feel devalued and put it on ourselves.

Thankfully, God has the power and delight to deliver us and help us to live in truth. If we have done something wrong, we can deal with our sin by confessing it to God, owning up to what He already knows. Then restoration can come.

We can also get rid of shame as we allow the Lord to replace the darkness of fear and embarrassment with His love and truth about who we really are. Truth brings light, and radiance! "I sought the Lord, and he answered me; he delivered me from all my fears. Those who look to him are radiant; their faces are never covered with shame" (Psalm 34:4–5).

Blame, on the other hand, says, "It's your fault," and puts the wrong done on another person, holding them responsible for their wrongdoings sometimes for months or years. You may also blame yourself for what went wrong in the relationship.

Years ago I held on to blame for a long time after a heart-wrenching breakup. My line of thinking went something like this: "It's his fault I'm so miserable; he broke up with me. If he wouldn't have left, I wouldn't be so sad. And if I wasn't so sad, I wouldn't have eaten so much junk food. If I wouldn't have eaten all this garbage, I would be much thinner. So basically it's his fault that I've gained weight." The twisting path to destructive thinking had begun, and it was not a good thing.

A few years later I was still nursing a grudge against this man because I didn't know how to let it go. I was in a hotel room in Denver getting dressed for the day when I heard a television preacher say, "When are you going to stop blaming someone else for their poor choices?" I froze in my tracks. The words were a holy "aha" moment. Sure, he had made poor choices that messed things up in my life. But as a result, I made my own bad decisions and I was blaming him for it all. I finally realized that it was time to take responsibility for my own actions and learn to make better choices in my future relationships and in my life.

FEEL THE PAIN, OR IT REMAINS

In *The Wounded Woman*, Dr. Steve Stephens and Pam Vredevelt say, "Denying, stuffing, or numbing our feelings with some sort of addictive behavior only prolongs or intensifies our pain. It blocks us from moving forward."[1] The authors use the example of trying to keep a beach ball underwater. You may try to hold it down, but it always forces its way back up. "Repressing our feelings may give us a sense of protection," they continue, "but it requires a tremendous amount of energy."[2]

> KNOW THE difference between experiencing your feelings and being led by them.

Stephens concludes, "Allowing feelings to come to the surface can bring healing and provide us with the extra energy we need to rebuild our life."[3] As difficult as it can be, feeling your feelings, "experiencing them," eventually releases the pain. Held in, the pain remains. Like a deep tissue massage for back pain, it may hurt while the therapist is working on you, but it feels much better later on as the pain is released. It's the kind of hurt that heals.

At the same time, it's important to *know the difference between experiencing your feelings and being led by them.* Apart from God, we can let our feelings take control and that almost always makes the situation worse. Even as believers we have a continual need to feed our minds truth instead of being misshapen by popular culture or negative self-talk.

That's why it's so essential to know God's Word. When the time comes to respond, you know that you serve a higher authority and you can "take captive every thought to make it obedient to Christ" (2 Corinthians 10:5), which means you have the *choice* to entertain those thoughts or not.

For instance, after your last breakup the temptation to get back at your old boyfriend may be strong. You may want revenge because of how he lied, cheated, and stole your heart. You want payback. But just because you feel that way, doesn't mean you have to let those thoughts linger or act on them.

Just as you would get an unruly guest out of your home, you have every right to throw unwanted thoughts out of your head. Usher them out with God's truth which will give you all the resources you need—His strength, power, and wisdom—to do what is right instead of what you feel.

LET GO OF FALSE BELIEFS

Whether you feel angry, rejected, fearful, or any other emotions, you can choose what you want to do with them; your feelings don't have to control you. In fact, one of the biggest keys to processing emotional pain is learning to separate truth from lies, and then living in God's truth. You can challenge false beliefs, reject lies, and choose to live in freedom instead of emotional bondage by recognizing the lies, releasing them, and then realizing and acting on the truth. Here are some common counterfeit things people may think after a breakup:

+ Lie: *I have less worth without a man.*
  Truth: Everyone longs for love, and that's a good and

healthy desire. But whether you are in a relationship or not, you have infinite worth and value.

+ Lie: *I must have this person in order to be happy.*
Truth: When you put another person before God, you risk making the one you loved into an idol, or what John Eldredge in *Desire* calls a Golden Person (your longing for a soul-to-soul connection "something at the level of *worship*").[4]

+ Lie: *He is "mine."*
Truth: You don't own anyone. The person you loved belongs to God; he is not yours.

+ Lie: *I am a victim.*
Truth: You may have suffered emotional wounds, but you don't have to have a victim mind-set. You may not have had a choice in this matter, but you have choices now—and that can give you hope.

+ Lie: *My life is over.*
Truth: While your relationship with another person has ended, it's not the end of the world, and it's not the end of you.

RELEASE EVERYTHING TO GOD

After a breakup a few years ago with the man I thought I'd marry, I was having a hard time letting go, and my friend Tammy gave me some sage advice: "You've got to die to it." She was talking about surrendering your own personal agenda and submitting it to God.

And then I remembered that the Christian experience is a life of continual surrender, not giving up but yielding to the Spirit.

Despite my hurting heart, God was still in control. He knew what was best for my love life because He loved me and knew me better than I knew myself. Hard as it was, it was time to release this relationship—what I wanted—so I could move forward.

Letting go is hard. We may think God will drop the ball, but He never drops the ball. We may fear not being in control. Maybe we're afraid of the empty hands we'll have when we release the little we try to possess. By not releasing the relationship or the emotional pain to God, we are essentially saying, "I don't trust You. My way is better. I know best."

When we surrender our will, we learn to rely on God totally and trust that He has something better suited for us and that He will provide. As you *release* your grip on whatever it is that you are holding to so tightly, and *replace* it with Jesus (and His unchanging truth), He will *restore* your weary, wayward, or willful heart and lead you to brighter days.

Some people mistakenly think that surrender equals weakness. Instead, giving God your all takes incredible courage and strength. It is brave. You are releasing with a vision of what letting go can become.

A good example of releasing and restoration is found in Psalm 126:5–6, "Those who sow in tears will reap with songs of joy. He who goes out weeping, carrying seed to sow, will return with songs of joy, carrying sheaves with him." As you surrender your heart to God, incredible transformation can happen.

Think of the amazing transformation that takes place, too, when wheat seeds surrender to the soil. It is a journey of continual surrender as small seeds transform into mature plants, and then are harvested, bundled, and made into flour, which you buy at the store and take home to make bread.

As you knead the dough, the little pieces of wheat submit to a new form. After punching and rising, punching and rising, the dough—*pounded for a purpose*—surrenders to the intense heat of the oven and there it is changed into what it was meant to be.

Finally, as you open the oven and take out the baked dough, the delightful aroma of fresh baked bread fills the kitchen. You've taken something in its raw form and shaped it into something it wasn't—just as God does with us.

Will you surrender your breakup and your emotions to God, and let Him transform your heartache to joy? As you release the lies and replace them with truth, He will restore.

PRAYER

Lord, I have so many emotions swirling in my head right now. Please help me. Would You show me how to best deal with the anger I feel? Heal my broken heart from this rejection. Teach me how to battle fear and win. Help me to let go of false beliefs and soak in Your truth. Lord, You are the One I turn to because You have the power to make real and lasting changes in my life. I surrender this pain, and trust You for restoration. In Jesus' name, Amen.

LIGHT FOR THE JOURNEY

Light overcomes darkness. Here are some key verses—the light of God's Word—to carry with you or memorize so you can be prepared when deception or lies threaten. Remember, it's one thing to know a lot of Bible verses, it's quite another to let them change your life. James 1:22 and 25 remind us to "do" the Word, to live it out not just know it; then we will find freedom and be blessed.

Do not merely listen to the word, and so deceive yourselves. Do what it says. (James 1:22)

But the man who looks intently into the perfect law that gives freedom, and continues to do this, not forgetting what he has heard, but doing it—he will be blessed in what he does. (James 1:25)

For I am the Lord, your God, who takes hold of your right hand and says to you, Do not fear; I will help you. (Isaiah 41:13)

The Lord's right hand has done mighty things! I will not die but live, and will proclaim what the Lord has done. (Psalm 118:16–17)

O Lord my God, I called to you for help and you healed me. (Psalm 30:2)

For nothing is impossible with God. (Luke 1:37)

ILLUMINATION

1. Do you feel like you have a right to your feelings? Why or why not?

2. Dealing with your emotions is essential to healing your broken heart. What emotions are you feeling right now (hurt, pain, anger, betrayal, sadness, bitterness, or other emotions)?

3. How does God help us handle emotions?

4. This chapter stated, "As you release your grip on whatever it is that you are holding to so tightly, and replace it with Jesus (and His unchanging truth), He will restore your weary, wayward, or willful heart and lead you to brighter days." What is one thing you can do this week to release or replace?

5 Night Lights: Experiencing God's Love

Let him who walks in the dark, who has no light,
trust in the name of the Lord and rely on his God.
—Isaiah 50:10

One summer day Chad and I had taken a late after-noon walk in a wooded area a few miles from his house. I had been so engaged in our conversation that I hadn't noticed it was getting dark. Soon it was pitch black—at least it seemed that way to me. Yet we walked on.

I had no idea how we were going to get back to the car with-out a flashlight—but Chad had walked these trails many times, even at night, and he knew them well. So he confidently walked the trail in front of me as I held on tightly to him. With his pres-ence and woodland wisdom I was less afraid. Nearly an hour later we arrived safely back at his car and drove away.

I needed a trail guide that night to get me through an intensely dark time. I had to trust and rely on someone who knew where he was going and could lead me safely home even when I could not see the way.

Isn't it reassuring to know that God can see in the dark even when you cannot? Psalm 139:12 reminds us, " Even the darkness will not be dark to you; the night will shine like the day, for *dark-ness is as light to you*" (emphasis mine). God knows where you are all the time. In the midnight hour and in the noonday sun He sees, He knows, He cares, and He will lead you through the dark-ness of your heartbreak and into healing—into brighter days.

ERICA'S STORY

Knowing *about* God is one thing; knowing His close presence and trusting Him is quite another. Erica learned a lot about trust-ing God after a significant relationship ended in an unexpected and hurtful way.

It looked like Erica's dream of the perfect marriage to a godly man would come true when she became engaged to Wayne, a

Bible college student in her town. Even her pastor had told them that if ever two people were meant to be together, it was them.

Sadly, things began to unravel shortly after the wedding ceremony. On her wedding night, Wayne didn't even kiss her. He also confessed that he no longer desired to pray together and that his faith was not what he originally said it meant to him.

Erica was shocked and devastated, but she had hope that things would change. "I thought that if I prayed hard enough and did the right things, our relationship would be different," she said.

Though she prayed fervently for her marriage and sought advice from godly leaders, Erica continued to experience rejection from her husband on a regular basis. So she coped by throwing herself into her work; and while her career flourished, her marriage floundered. "People thought we had the perfect marriage," said Erica, "but behind closed doors, my heart was broken."

For years, she prayed for healing in the relationship. Wayne cycled in and out of attending church, and her hopes soared and crashed each time. When Wayne didn't desire a physical relationship, Erica often wondered what was wrong with her.

Then, after twelve years of marriage, she discovered that Wayne had been living a double life. Unbeknownst to Erica, Wayne had worked hard to cover up deeper issues, including illegal activity, for years.

Despite all that, Erica dug in even harder to save her marriage. She sought out a Christian counselor, read books on marriage recovery, and with the support of her counselor, church leadership, and caring friends, started implementing tough love with Wayne.

Unfortunately, he chose to leave and filed for divorce. Wayne had given her a simple choice: choose him and join his anti-God lifestyle, or choose God. She chose God. And while she knew it was the right thing to do, Erica's heart felt like it split in two.

After thirteen years of persistent effort, she was ultimately rejected. "It was hard to let go of the dream that Wayne would love me," said Erica. "I cried for months. But I came to learn that while I *loved*, I could not control the *outcome* of that love."

Getting from denial to acceptance of the truth took a long time. During the next several months, Erica began to awaken to the fact that even though their relationship ended, there was more to the rest of her life. She learned that endings are really new beginnings, and as we grieve, we eventually get through the process and find acceptance; we are able to move on.

One thing that helped her get into the light of hope again was reading devotions about God's character. "Focusing on that really helped me to know Him and better trust Him," said Erica. "Even when things around me seemed to be falling apart, I wanted to know, 'Who is this Person who has my life in His hands? Who knew all of my days before there was yet one of them? Who is this all-knowing One who works all things together for my good and His glory?'"

Erica was referring to three comforting Bible verses:

My times are in your hands. (Psalm 31:15)

All the days ordained for me were written in your book before one of them came to be. (Psalm 139:16)

And we know that in all things God works for the good of those who love him, who have been called according to his purpose. (Romans 8:28)

It felt like midnight in Erica's life—dark, devastating, and uncertain. However, through her heart-healing journey she longed to know more about the One who was leading her through the night and into the sunrise, into joy.

During a relationship or after it ends, you may have your own questions that need illumination, like: "Why did this breakup happen?" or "Where is God in all of this?" You may trip over doubt and stumble over confusion as you wonder how you could ever trust yourself, trust others, or even trust God again because you thought the man who left was the one you were supposed to be with—perhaps forever. How do you rebuild trust despite unanswered "whys" and when you simply do not understand?

LEARNING FROM LOSS

A man named Job got the biggest wake-up call of his life and learned deeper levels of knowing and trusting God through an ordeal like no other. He was an honest man, with a heart devoted to God. He had a wife and ten children, and was extremely wealthy. You can read the story in the Bible's book of Job.

Things were happening in the unseen world and it played out in Job's life. In essence, the Evil One had a conversation with God saying that Job had it good in life now, but he would curse God and turn away from Him if all his blessings were taken away. God agreed that Job could be tested.

Job's world was rocked when he learned that foreigners had attacked and carried away some of his children, his flocks and servants were burned with fire, and the roof of his house collapsed and all of his other children perished. In utter grief, Job fell to the ground and worshiped. He said, "'The Lord gave and the Lord has taken away; may the name of the Lord be praised.' In all this, Job did not sin by charging God with wrongdoing" (Job 1:21–22).

But the tests kept coming. He developed painful sores all over his body, and his wife even told him to turn his back on God. She said, "Are you still holding on to your integrity? Curse God and die!" (Job 2:9). In other words, give up. It's too much for anyone to handle. Still, Job did not sin with his words.

Three of his friends came to visit Job to comfort him, and he cried out in his misery. But while his friends sympathized with him, they spoke incorrectly when they told him that he must have sinned in order for God to be so mad at him and punish him with these trials.

Then Job had some very dark days. He became overwhelmingly sad and began to give up entirely. Hope had faded. He complained about his circumstances and thought that he would never be happy again. It simply made no sense to Job why his entire life had crumbled around him.

Despite his innocence, Job suffered greatly. Yet he was unaware of what was really happening. Just as gold is refined by intense heat, the heat was on in Job's life. Through the losses, lack, physical pain, embarrassment, and more, this good, honest man was being tested and refined.

Finally, Job prayed and poured out his heart and troubles to God. And God spoke, confronting Job's ignorance with an "Are you questioning Me and My ways?" speech as He reveals His majesty and greatness as the One who created the world and holds it all together.

God asked, "Where were you when I laid the earth's foundation? Tell me, if you understand" (Job 38:4) and divulged a litany of examples. Here are just a few:

Have you ever given orders to the morning, or shown the dawn its place[?] (Job 38:12)

What is the way to the abode of light? And where does darkness reside? (Job 38:19)

Do you send the lightning bolts on their way? Do they report to you, "Here we are?" (Job 38:35)

Does the eagle soar at your command and build his nest on

high? (Job 39:27)

Humbled and amazed, Job answered back. "Then Job replied to the Lord: 'I know that you can do all things; no plan of yours can be thwarted. You asked, "Who is this that obscures my counsel without knowledge?" Surely I spoke of things I did not understand, things too wonderful for me to know. You said, "Listen now, and I will speak; I will question you, and you shall answer me." *My ears had heard of you but now my eyes have seen you.* Therefore I despise myself and repent in dust and ashes'" (Job 42:1–6, emphasis mine).

Job had heard *about* God, but now he had *experienced* the Lord firsthand and he was never the same again.

> YOU MAY not be able to
> perceive what God is doing
> in your life right now, but perhaps,
> like Job, your question of "Why?"
> will turn to "Who?" as you
> draw nearer to the One who
> has the answers.

Job had wrestled with God's words against his own harsh reality. He listened as God unveiled His divine nature. And he came to a place, despite his adversity, of connecting with the all-knowing, mighty, and powerful God. In awe and reverence he realized that Love was there all along. God was still protecting him and, in His mercy, God restored Job's life.

In the end, goodness and justice shone through. Job was restored to health, comforted by his extended family, and was blessed more in the second half of his life than the first. In fact, he had ten more children, tens of thousands of livestock, and lived 140 more years!

Most likely, your breakup wasn't as bad as Job's horrible time of testing. But whether you were simply disappointed or downright devastated, you may also be wrestling with your own ideas about God's character. You may not be able to perceive what God is doing in your life right now, but perhaps, like Job, your question of "Why?" will turn to "Who?" as you draw nearer to the One who has the answers. As you come to know God more and trust Him, you realize the One who takes care of the vast universe and all that is in it, also has His hands—and heart—on you.

In the darkest time of Job's life he learned to see with new eyes as he *experienced* God, beholding Him and coming to a place of radical life transformation.

"So often our primary ambition is to escape pain or feel good or be delivered from a problem when instead we need to keep our focus on the big picture of what God is doing in our life and the lives of others through pain or problems," writes Anne Graham Lotz in *Why?* "Our principle aim," she continues, "should be to glorify God, not to be honored or to be healthy or to be happy."[1]

Of course, being happy or healthy is not a bad thing; it's just not the first thing. Often we do not understand what God is up to because, well, He is God. And we are not. There will always be an element of mystery in why God does what He does; we will never have all the answers this side of heaven. But we can rest assured that the One who loves us most, will reveal all that we need to know when we need to know it. And that is enough.

Many times I've grappled with my own "Why?" questions after a breakup. Over time, a lot of prayer and many tears later, I finally came to a place where I remembered and acknowledged God's sovereignty; He is in control even when circumstances are confusing. After holding so tightly to what I thought I wanted, I could, in humble surrender, say, "I do not understand, Lord, but I will trust You." I learned that He is wiser than I am, He knows best, and He will provide for my heart-connection needs—whatever that looks like.

God is okay with our questions as we wrestle with our will and His way. In the struggle, He is building strength. It is here that we learn to know Him and really trust His heart. "Trust in the Lord with all your heart and lean not on your own understanding; in all your ways acknowledge him, and he will make your paths straight" (Proverbs 3:5–6).

TO KNOW IS TO TRUST

In a relationship, the more you know someone, the more you can trust him. The same is true with God. The more we *know* God, the more we *trust* Him. However, many of us have distorted images of what God is really like. Because of our own ignorance, a pastor's misrepresentation, childhood issues, or other reasons, we may think God is something He is not.

Many years ago I pictured God sitting with His back to me in a very large leather executive chair. He was not to be bothered, except in extremely urgent circumstances. If I did approach Him, it was with fear and trembling because He was very busy and had many more important things to attend to than my requests. It was my thought that if you talked to God and He swirled around to face you in His oversized chair, you had to say what you needed to say very fast and very succinctly. Expect a short but wise answer, and get out of there as fast as you can.

I know better now.

When you only guess at what God is like, it's like standing in the shadows instead of basking in the warm glow of God's love.

Away from the fire, like loving Him from a distance, it's cold and dim. But God invites you to come closer—from the chill of detachment into the kindness, affection, attention, and powerful love of the One who loves you most.

"On a daily basis we're faced with two simple choices," says C. J. Mahaney, president of Sovereign Grace Ministries. "We can either *listen* to ourselves and our constantly changing feelings about our circumstances, or we can *talk* to ourselves about the unchanging truth of who God is and what He's accomplished for us at the cross. Far too often we choose to passively listen to ourselves. We sit back and let our view of God and life be shaped by our constantly shifting feelings about our ever-changing circumstances."[2]

We need to know "the unchanging truth of who God is and what He's accomplished for us"—the true character of the One who "reveals the deep things of darkness and brings deep shadows into the light" (Job 12:22).

GOD'S TRUE CHARACTER

Night has its own beauty and purpose. In the evening sky, against a backdrop of darkness, God provides night lights like the moon, the stars, and the spectacular glow of the aurora borealis, the northern lights. Have you ever looked up at an enormous harvest moon, round and brilliant, that was so bright the night appeared almost like day? Or looked up at the Big Dipper, connected the stars with your eyes, and recognized the saucepan shape? Certainly, "the heavens declare the glory of God" (Psalm 19:1).

In your own personal nighttime—when you feel sad, lonely, or in angst over lost love or dating defeats—God provides light for the way to your new beginning. When you know more about who God is (His character), what He has done and is doing even now, then your response to Him and to your circumstances changes dramatically. To experience God's amazing ways on deeper levels we need to remember who He is and "forget not all his benefits" (Psalm 103:2). As we look to what God says about Himself in His Word, the Holy Bible, our trust will be an informed, not a blind trust.

The night lights God provides are innumerable—His absolute love, tender mercy, healing grace, and guiding wisdom, just to name a few. But perhaps the brightest "light" of God's character is His love.

THE LIGHT OF UNCONDITIONAL LOVE

God's love is amazing. Because He cared so much for you and me, He sent His Son, Jesus Christ, to earth. For three years Jesus demonstrated ultimate kindness and compassion, healed the sick, performed miracles, and taught people how to live in God-honoring ways.

He had a purpose for being here; in His death and resurrection on a wooden cross, God's mission was fulfilled. Because the cross is empty and the tomb He once occupied is vacant, we can live free forever.

Despite our failures and imperfections (yes, even without makeup on) God accepts us. No matter who you are or what you've done, God's radical, unconditional love and forgiveness reach everyone. We just need to make the choice to reach back. And when we do, we discover that love changes everything.

When God shows us love has limits, we may think He is being unkind, when in reality He is working things out for our benefit. For instance, when you want the answer to be "yes" and God says "no," that doesn't mean He loves you less. It means He is wiser; He knows what we don't know, and as a loving Father, He protects us and keeps us on track.

God loves us, and He asks for our love in return. When the religious experts of Jesus' day asked Him which commandment was the greatest, He answered with two: "'Love the Lord your God with all your heart and with all your soul and with all your mind.'

This is the first and greatest commandment. And the second is like it: 'Love your neighbor as yourself'" (Matthew 22:37, 38).

Loving others is not as challenging when we are replenished with the love of God in us. When we are filled up with God's love, we are not as frantic, fearful, or frustrated in relationships or breakups. A calm knowing settles in so we can be ourselves, accept people as they are, and not try to control things all the time. We can cease striving.

When God's incredible love fills us first, we are not starving for love and approval from others and that helps us to make better choices in the people we date or eventually marry. Max Lucado says, "When you know God loves you, you won't be desperate for the love of others."[3]

NIGHT LIGHTS OF GOD'S CHARACTER

Just as the stars in the night sky are countless, so the attributes of God are innumerable. Some of the other incredible things about God include:

His justice (Isaiah 30:18)
His forgiveness (Luke 7:48)
His mercy (Lamentations 3:22–23)
His grace (Ephesians 2:8)
His compassion (Psalm 103:13)
His comfort (Psalm 94:19)
His wisdom (1 Corinthians 1:20–30)
His guidance (Psalm 43:3)
His freedom (John 8:36)
His healing (1 Peter 2:24)
His goodness (Psalm 145:9)
His holiness (Psalm 99:5)
His majesty (Exodus 15:11)
His hope (Psalm 62:5)

His provision (Matthew 6:25–26)
His protection (Psalm 4:8)
His power and authority (Matthew 28:18–19)
His peace (John 14:27)

CONNECTING WITH GOD

Because of God's grace and forgiveness, we are undone. Because of His holiness, we are in awe of Him and reverence Him. Because of His goodness, we are overjoyed!

It is difficult to contain in a single chapter the extent of all God is and all He has accomplished since entire books have been written on His attributes. Indeed, there are not enough words to describe His wonder.

But as we come to know more about God and experience Him in our daily lives, trust is built and a connection grows. We are no longer living from our head but from our heart. When we *experience* God—when we truly connect—we are never the same. Neither is the world around us.

How can we connect with God?

As you *read God's words in the Bible*, He illuminates your thinking with wisdom and insight, and your heart with deeper love. "Your word is a lamp to my feet and a light for my path" (Psalm 119:105).

As you *pray*, your prayers change circumstances, people, and attitudes; they change you. In my book *Power Prayers for Women*, I offer that prayer is a love connection with God. "Prayer connects us to the One who has the power to make lasting changes in our lives. It's a holy conversation, talking and listening to God Almighty, the One who loves us more than we will ever know. In fact, that's where the power in powerful prayers comes from: being connected."[4]

Prayer connects us to the One who has the power to make lasting changes in our lives.

> PRAYER CONNECTS us
> to the One who has the
> power to make lasting
> changes in our lives.

As you *worship*, your heart is changed. Whether you sing praise songs in church or harmonize with a music CD in your car, worship draws you near in a unique way as you are transported from sorrow to joy, from darkness to light. "From the rising of the sun to the place where it sets, the name of the Lord is to be praised" (Psalm 113:3). We worship God because He is worthy.

When Erica's husband left, she found it comforting and healing to listen to worship CDs. "It helped me focus on God's love for me as I fell asleep each night. The Holy Spirit would comfort me as I listened, and it played a significant part in my healing."

Connection leads to transformation. When we engage, not ignoring God or taking Him for granted, we are renewed and exceedingly thankful.

The purpose of knowing God's attributes is to form a deeper relationship, a bond. Then, as we come to know His heart and His goodness, we can experience authentic community, real healing, and true love. We come to trust that He is more than able and very willing to take care of us. We can say with the apostle Paul, "I know whom I have believed, and am convinced that he is able to guard what I have entrusted to him for that day" (2 Timothy 1:12).

I know. I'm convinced. He is able.

My prayer is that the Lord will continue to reveal Himself to you as you seek to put Him first and follow. "I keep asking that the God of our Lord Jesus Christ, the glorious Father, may give you the Spirit of wisdom and revelation, *so that you may know him better*" (Ephesians 1:17, emphasis mine).

When you do, the Holy Spirit may just surprise you by empowering you to do things you never thought you could—like forgiving someone who's hurt you. Or even forgiving yourself.

PRAYER

Lord, I want to know You and experience more of Your character. Help me to learn from my losses and live by Your unchanging truth. Reveal to me more about Your mercy and justice so I can forgive others and be forgiven. I want to experience Your compassion and comfort and learn more of Your majesty, holiness, and hope. Lord, show me how to connect with You and experience love like I have never known. Thank You for Your never-ending love for me. In Jesus' name, Amen.

LIGHT FOR THE JOURNEY

Though I sit in darkness, the Lord will be my light. (Micah 7:8)

Yet the Lord longs to be gracious to you; he rises to show you compassion. For the Lord is a God of justice. Blessed are all who wait for him! (Isaiah 30:18)

Because of the Lord's great love we are not consumed, for his compassions never fail. They are new every morning; great is your faithfulness. (Lamentations 3:22–23)

For it is by grace you have been saved, through faith—and this not from yourselves, it is the gift of God— not by works, so that no one can boast. (Ephesians 2:8)

Trust in the Lord with all your heart and lean not on your own understanding; in all your ways acknowledge him, and he will make your paths straight. (Proverbs 3:5–6)

I know whom I have believed, and am convinced that he is able to guard what I have entrusted to him for that day. (2 Timothy 1:12)

ILLUMINATION

1. How does Job's story of loss and restoration encourage you?

2. How do you "picture" God?

3. What is one aspect of God's character that means a lot to you?

4. What are some new ways you can connect with God this week?

Out of the
Shadows:
6 # Discovering
the Power of
Forgiveness

To be a Christian means to forgive the inexcusable,
because God has forgiven the inexcusable in you.
—C. S. Lewis

It was a cold Colorado day in January and the world was covered in white. As I walked along admiring the contrast of the deep blue sky and red orange rocks against the pure white snow, I saw something that made me stop in my tracks. It was a scrub oak with lifeless leaves still hanging on to the tree. *How odd,* I thought, as the winter wind blew snow off the brown crunchy leaves. *Autumn is over. Why are they still holding on to this tree when their season has passed?* The dried-up leaves clung to the swaying branches as if their life depended on it. Only they were dead.

And then it dawned on me. That's exactly what I'd been doing. Like the brown crunchy oak leaves, I'd been holding on to last season; my heart was stuck in the past. What would it take to finally let go?

Truthfully, the relationship had been dead for months. I knew in my head that it was over, but my heart refused to agree. This guy had wanted my time and attention for almost two years, and never had any intention of marrying me. How could I excuse those lost years? Behind my back, he started dating a woman who was a good friend of mine. He said he never wanted kids, and now he's married and has a few of them. I knew I needed to forgive him, and forgive myself for my own foolish choices in the relationship, but how could I?

As I stood there, the wind suddenly picked up and some of the dead leaves blew off the branches, releasing their stubborn grip. At that moment I realized I needed a stronger force to help me release what I was grasping so tightly. I needed the power of the Holy Spirit to blow a fresh breeze into my life and enable me to do what I could not do. Let go. Release. Forgive.

Henri Nouwen once said, "When a wound is healed, there still can be some leftover pain."[1] Getting over someone who's dumped you can be harder for some people than others, especially if you've experienced emotional wounds in your past. You may not be conscious of it, but pain from long ago is still there, deep in your heart, and that can make it difficult to let go of pain in the present. Perhaps your parents divorced when you were a child and you've never gotten healing from the initial feeling of abandonment, a feeling which is echoed or deepened by a breakup. Or maybe your best friend in grade school rejected you to start hanging out with the "cool" kids in junior high leaving you to feel discarded. An earlier pain is making its way into your present pain.

Left-behind pain comes in all sorts of ways. It could be due to a divorce (your parents or your own), a death in the family, a family member's illness, a rape, or abuse (physical, sexual, or emotional). Even little hurts and repeated disappointments can pile up and turn into a mountain of resentment. The bottom line is: "Something in your past is unresolved and therefore still has a hold on you," says Neil T. Anderson in *Victory Over the Darkness*.[2]

Anderson, founder and president of Freedom in Christ Ministries, calls "the residual effect of past traumas *primary emotions*."[3] In fact, he continues, "The intensity of your primary emotions is determined by your previous life history. The more traumatic your experience, the more intense will be your primary emotion."[4]

According to Anderson, an event in the present can set off something inside you that may have been dormant for years. A relationship breakup, for instance, could activate emotions like intense anger or extreme feelings of rejection, and you may be puzzled as to why you are reacting the way you do—and why you can't let go. Realizing that the past is spilling over into your present will help you to deal with it.

In order to find resolution, it's important to know that you are no longer a prisoner of your past. You can see things differently through the eyes of an adult, or as someone who is further from the trauma of the past. "You have the privilege of evaluating your past experience in the light of who you are today, as opposed to who you were then," said Anderson.[5]

As you begin to see with new eyes how other hurts can affect your current breakup pain, you can then take one of the most essential steps to heal your heart: forgive those who have offended you.

FORGIVENESS IS THE KEY TO HEALING

A major key that heals brokenness after a relationship ends is forgiveness—whether it's forgiving past pain, forgiving the person who hurt you in the present, or forgiving yourself. "Forgiveness," according to Dan Allender and Tremper Longman III in *Bold Love* "is the light that penetrates the dark and frees the somber, shamed heart to leap with love."[6]

Whether the offense was in the past or the present, holding on to that pain not only continues to hurt you, it can also block you from moving forward. The pent-up pain turns into bitterness, resentment, or offense and the emotional poison can work its way into other areas of your life. With pride, ignorance, or sheer selfishness we stubbornly cling, like those brown crunchy leaves, to what we want or what we think should happen. "He is wrong, and I'm right." "I want justice (or revenge)." "What he did was inexcusable."

YOU DON'T OWE ME

Years ago at a singles retreat in Green Lake, Wisconsin, Andy Stanley gave a talk on the topic of forgiveness. I remember him saying something to the effect that when you do not forgive, it's as if you hold that person hostage in your heart. You take them out once in a while, beat them up, and put them back.

When you feel wronged, you think the other person owes you

something. They owe you an apology, an explanation, a childhood, a relationship, or a marriage. Whatever it is, you are holding them prisoner, but you are the one with the pain. Then Stanley opened his hands, and with his palms turned up, told us that forgiveness means we release that person and say, "You don't owe me."

How do you go from a place where you feel someone is emotionally indebted to you to a place you can release and forgive? Often people find it difficult to forgive because they don't know what it means.

WHAT FORGIVENESS IS . . . AND IS NOT

Forgiveness is not forgetting about what happened or acting like everything is okay. It does not mean that you condone what happened, agree with it, or like it. You are not excusing the offense, and you are definitely not letting the offender off the hook for their words or actions. Instead, you're putting them on God's hook, and trusting God to deal with it fairly because He said He would. As you release the person who's wronged you to God, *He* ensures justice is served; not you. "Do not take revenge, my friends, but leave room for God's wrath, for it is written: 'It is mine to avenge; I will repay,' says the Lord" (Romans 12:19).

I like what C. D. Baker says about God's justice in *40 Loaves: Breaking Bread with Our Father Each Day*: "Yes, God seeks justice and so should we. He grieves when we are oppressed or taken advantage of, and he demands justice on our behalf. But what we forget is that *Jesus* already paid the price for others' violations against us . . . and for our violations against them. *We* don't need to seek vengeance"[7] (emphasis mine). Indeed, the God of unconditional love is also our advocate for justice.

Forgiveness is not judging another. Matthew 7:1–3 reads, "Do not judge, or you too will be judged. For in the same way you judge others, you will be judged, and with the measure you use, it will be measured to you. Why do you look at the speck of sawdust in your brother's eye and pay no attention to the plank in your own eye?"

The simple fact is none of us knows the true motives in another's heart. We don't excuse or condone bad behavior, but it's not for us to judge. That's God's job. "Therefore judge nothing before the appointed time; wait till the Lord comes. He will bring to light what is hidden in darkness and will expose the motives of men's hearts. At that time each will receive his praise from God" (1 Corinthians 4:5).

Forgiveness is not dependent upon the other person. If you have been wronged and the other person repents, and asks for forgiveness because he is truly sorry, the Bible commands us to forgive. "Bear with each other and forgive whatever grievances you may have against one another. Forgive as the Lord forgave you" (Colossians 3:13). That doesn't mean you are obligated to be his friend or marry him. You can choose how to relate to him in the future but, as you will see later in this chapter, forgiveness does not always lead to reconciliation.

What if the other person is not repentant? In an ideal world, the person who has wronged you would come forward and say he was sorry. He'd acknowledge his wrongdoing and ask for forgiveness. In an ideal world a lot of things would be different. But our willingness to forgive is not dependent upon the other person.

Despite our soul wounds, we are called, as Christian believers, to follow Christ's example. On the cross, Jesus prayed for those who harmed Him, "Father, forgive them, for they do not know what they are doing" (Luke 23:34). Yes, it's hard to forgive someone who's hurt you, but we do not treat others as their sins deserve. In forgiving others you are not erasing their wrongdoings or the consequences they will incur. You are taking your pain to Jesus and giving it to Him. And it sets *your* heart free.

Forgiveness is not a one-time thing. When Peter came to Jesus and asked how many times he should forgive a brother who sins against him, Peter thought he was being generous when he offered to forgive up to seven times. Jesus' reply must have startled Peter when Jesus said seventy times seven (Matthew 18:21–22). We forgive again and again, but we are also wise as to how we let the other person treat us.

Forgiveness comes in time, not always right away. Sometimes we have to grieve it first, and pray that we can feel it. Worship leader Ross Parsley once said, "Forgiveness is a decision, but healing is a process."

Forgiving others is possible, and you can come into a gradually brighter light of understanding how to do so as you:

+ **Acknowledge you have been hurt.** "I have been wronged."
+ **Receive God's forgiveness.** "I have been wrong, too. I need forgiveness."
+ **Choose to forgive.** "I'm wrestling with why I should forgive him."
+ **Release to God in prayer—and forgive.** "Because God has forgiven me, I will forgive him."

ACKNOWLEDGE YOU HAVE BEEN HURT

For some people this is obvious. You know you have been wounded with words or actions, and it is clear to you. Others may have a harder time recognizing or admitting anything happened. For whatever reason, they don't want to deal with the issues; they want to deny the offense so there is no need for forgiveness.

While you may have been offended, that does not mean you have to hold on to the offense. In this life we will be hurt or offended many times; that's a given. However, we have the choice of how we respond to the wrongdoing.

John Bevere in *The Bait of Satan: Living Free from the Deadly Trap of Offense*, says that offense is a tool used by the Enemy to bring believers into captivity leaving them ensnared and unable to break free. "Pride keeps you from dealing with truth," says Bevere. "It distorts your vision. You never change when you think everything is fine."[8] You hold on to the offense, so you hold back forgiveness.

> WHILE YOU MAY have been offended, that does not mean you have to hold on to the offense.

Just as you plant seeds in your garden and reap a harvest of summer fruits and vegetables, when you sow seeds of unconditional love you reap the love of God in your own life. And that love gives you the reason—and the power—to release the person who has wounded you. "The love of God is the key to freedom from the baited trap of offense," says Bevere.[9]

RECEIVE GOD'S FORGIVENESS

After you acknowledge that you have been hurt, it is helpful to ask yourself, "What is my part in this?" As the light of your own wrongdoing becomes brighter and you see the impact of your own behavior, you can begin to see more clearly the importance of forgiving others. We see the true condition of our own hearts and it helps us find the freedom forgiveness offers in our lives and in the lives of others.

As you consider your part in this relationship breakup, ask yourself, "Have I done anything wrong or hurtful in this situation?" Also, ask God in prayer to reveal to you how you can first look at your own stuff before you deal with the guy's wrongdoings toward you. Matthew 7:3 says, "Why do you look at the speck of sawdust in your brother's eye and pay no attention to the plank in your own eye?" Get forgiveness in your own life, and then you will be able to forgive others.

Receiving forgiveness from God begins when we realize that we need it. Until we do, we are spiritually "in the dark." Without the light of Christ in our lives, we are ignorant, prideful, self-centered, and often foolish. In fact, from early on in life we believe that everything revolves around us, until we learn that *we* revolve around *God*—just as people centuries ago discovered that the earth revolves around the sun, not the other way around.

The greatest darkness is being separated from the Source of light and life—not knowing God at all. As you hear God's truth and experience His love toward you, it illuminates your thinking and you begin to enter into God's freedom, forgiveness, pardon, and peace. Because of Jesus we become, like those in His day, "the people living in darkness [who] have seen a great light" (Matthew 4:16).

Jesus came to show us what God was like. It is a profound mystery, but God wanted all of mankind to know Him so we could connect with Him, be with Him. So He sent His Son, Jesus Christ. "For God, who said, 'Let light shine out of darkness,' made his light shine in our hearts to give us the light of the knowledge of the glory of God in the face of Christ" (2 Corinthians 4:6). Jesus, the Son, bears the image of God the Father. So when we are made right with Jesus—by receiving His forgiveness—we are in right standing with God. He is the connection. Our salvation. Our reconciliation.

A divine invitation. When a guest comes to your home and knocks on the front door, you open the door and let him in; you "receive" your guest. In the same way, we receive God's forgiveness when we open the door of our heart and allow Him in.

In Revelation 3:20, Jesus says, "Here I am! I stand at the door and knock. If anyone hears my voice and opens the door, I will come in and eat with him, and he with me." What would that be like?

Picture a room that is empty, gray, and cold, with sparse furniture. You are in that room and there is a knock on the door. You open the door a crack, leaving on the metal latch.

"Yes?"

It's Jesus. "May I come in?" He asks.

You think for a moment. *What does it really mean to let Him in? Should I open the door?*

You pause, and then decide to take a risk and open the latch. The moment He walks into the room it is instantly transformed. Suddenly, it is warm and wonderful. Life fills the room— a roaring fire in the fireplace, cushiony plump couches, and a sumptuous meal with the table set for dinner. You are awestruck. *Who is this One who fills my room, my life, with color, light, abundance, and life? What is this warmth and tender love?*

You sit at the table and feast on something succulent and heavenly. In the glow of the fire and the candles, Jesus leans back in His chair and smiles at you. You are still amazed at His goodness and kindness. You are relaxed and content. You smile back.

But then you become afraid because you think He will have to leave soon. It's so wonderful, and you want Him to stay.

He knows your thoughts even before you speak and assures you, "I'm not leaving. I will never leave. I will be with you always. And one day, you will come to My house and we'll live there forever." You breathe and relax again. *He is with me . . . always. Thank You, Lord.*

Jesus is knocking at the door of your heart. Will you open it?

Simply talk to Him about it in prayer; say what is on your heart in your own words and your own way. As you own up and confess what you've done wrong, ask God for forgiveness.

By God's grace, not by anything we have done, we can have spiritual deliverance, which is salvation. We are saved from sin through faith in Christ. It is His sacrificial love that gives our dead hearts life. Sin separates, but forgiveness reconnects us to the Father and brings us home.

Prodigal sons and daughters. Sometimes we get so off track that we wonder if we can ever come back. For some people, the words, "guilty, guilty, guilty" replay in their heads over and over again. Others, though, have no clue that they even need forgiveness. But God's forgiveness is greater than any sin.

Read Luke 15:11–32 for a glimpse of God's fathomless mercy through the story of the Prodigal Son. Jesus Himself told this story. It begins with a man who had two sons. The younger son asked his father for his part of the estate, his inheritance, and traveled to another country far away. There he spent his money recklessly in wild living, but he eventually ran out of resources and he was no longer wealthy; he was dirt poor.

After realizing his father's servants were better fed than he was, he returned home. He was humiliated, broken, and ashamed of his poor choices. And yet even when the young man was a long way off, the father saw him through the eyes of love. He ran to embrace him—perhaps he had been watching for him. He didn't scold or yell at him. He didn't say "Where were you?" or "What'd you do with all the money I gave you?"

The son knew he was wrong, and he didn't expect to be treated like anything more than a servant. But he was in for the surprise of his life. Because that day mercy not only walked, it ran to him. The father threw his arms around his long lost son and kissed him. He welcomed him home, and met him at the point of his greatest need—with love, not a lecture.

In our own ways, we are all prodigal sons or daughters. Just as the father welcomed home his wayward son with open arms, our heavenly Father treats us not as we deserve, but infinitely better. But it's up to us to make the choice and *receive* the love being showered upon us. "The Father's love does not force itself on the beloved," says Henri Nouwen in *The Return of the Prodigal Son*." Although he wants to heal us of all our inner darkness, we are still free to make our own choice to stay in the darkness or to step into the light of God's love."[10]

When we choose the light of God's love we can humbly and boldly come to Him and ask for forgiveness every time we need it. We can come with a repentant heart to God and He is always faithful to forgive. "If we confess our sins, he is faithful and just and will forgive us our sins and purify us from all unrighteousness" (1 John 1:9).

You may not always feel it right away, but you are forgiven. As you receive it, and continue to walk in freedom and not condemnation, the feelings will follow. You have the title, "Forgiven," now go live it.

CHOOSE TO FORGIVE

Sometimes we are wrong and we need forgiveness, and other times we are wronged; someone has hurt us. When they do, Christ wants us to forgive them. But before we can get to that place of release and forgiveness, we often wrestle with the decision. We want the other person to "get it," to understand how much he has hurt us. We may want him to pay or be punished for what he's done. The flesh (the human side of us) and the spirit part of us grapple with why we should forgive.

We may have myriad reasons to be hurt or angry, but our perspective changes when we realize what God has done for us. And in the light of the mercy He's shown us, we can extend the hand of forgiveness to others. To be sure, forgiveness does not always come easy. We want the scales of justice to be balanced; we want things to be fair. Yet, when we came to God asking Him for mercy despite our unwise and selfish ways, we were more than okay with the scales tipping in our favor.

Because He has first forgiven us, Christ commands us to forgive. And in an act of loving obedience to the One who loves us most we can follow Ephesians 4:31–32, "Get rid of all bitterness, rage and anger, brawling and slander, along with every form of malice. Be kind and compassionate to one another, forgiving each other, just as in Christ God forgave you."

Jesus Himself said, "For if you forgive men when they sin against you, your heavenly Father will also forgive you. But if you do not forgive men their sins, your Father will not forgive your sins" (Matthew 6:14–15).

Forgiveness is an act of your will; it is a choice. Choosing to forgive someone is a heart decision. You may still feel hurt or angry but you don't have to carry it around in your back pocket. Whether they ask for it or not, whether they change or not, choose to forgive.

> WHEN YOU forgive you
> are unbound and free to
> move into the next
> season of your life.

Forgiveness releases you. When you do not forgive, you are the one that hurts—physically and emotionally—not the other person. Don't let an unforgiving heart eat you up on the inside and destroy you. Whether it was ten years ago or ten days ago, when you forgive, you are unbound and free to move into the next season of your life. Forgiveness is the balm that heals the heart. When the pain has been dealt with, you can leave the past in the past. You don't have to drive on in life constantly looking in the rearview mirror. Because you are now moving forward, you look through the front windshield toward the future. Will you choose your way and hold on to the hurt, or God's way and forgive?

RELEASE TO GOD IN PRAYER—AND FORGIVE

Forgiveness is possible only by the grace of God. Author and pastor Robert Jeffress has a simple, yet effective, definition of grace. He says, "Grace is a deliberate decision to give something good to someone who doesn't deserve it."[11] God gives us the strength to release others to His justice, not ours.

You may find that you need to process the hurt before you are ready to forgive (see chapters 3 and 4 if you haven't already). Then, in prayer release the person who's wronged you and what they have done. There are two prayers at the end of the chapter that you can pray on your own, even out loud if you want, for forgiving others or finding it for yourself.

Forgiveness can eventually lead to acceptance. It takes time to integrate new ways of thinking into your heart and life. But in time, you will be able to come to a place of acceptance that the relationship is over and assimilate this new idea. It may not happen all at once. But acceptance will come, freeing you to live in reality and move forward.

Forgiveness does not always lead to reconciliation. It's important to understand that reconciliation is not always possible, wise, or safe. Certainly, we may long for a restored relationship with the person who's harmed us, or we may abhor the idea entirely. Either way, forgiveness "cancels the debt but does not lend new money until repentance occurs."[12]

In other words, "A forgiving heart opens the door to any who knock," according to Dan Allender and Tremper Longman III. "But entry into the home (that is, the heart) does not occur until the muddy shoes and dirty coat have been taken off. The offender must repent if true intimacy and reconciliation are ever to take place."[13]

Forgiveness does not mean we have to have a relationship or friendship with the other person or allow them to treat us badly. Use discernment to guard your heart and, unless they are truly repentant, stay away from a person who's harmed you.

Jasmine learned that forgiveness and reconciliation were two different things after a breakup a few years ago. Jasmine and Kurt had dated for about two years, but his anger was getting more and more out of control, escalating into physical and verbal abuse. Jasmine knew she had to get out of that unhealthy relationship.

One day, after they had finally broken up, a guest speaker at her church was speaking on the topic of forgiveness. It was incomprehensible to Jasmine how she could ever be able to forgive this violent man. But that day she learned that while Christ commands her to forgive, He did not require her to continue to be in a relationship with a man who showed no remorse. The pastor, with whom she spoke briefly after the service, assured her that it would be harmful, even dangerous, to see him, and Jasmine was relieved. In time, she did forgive him, but wisely chose to keep her distance.

FORGIVENESS LEADS TO FREEDOM AND PEACE

I never knew what freedom felt like until I was free. A person who has been forgiven much and who chooses to forgive others has a freed heart. No longer tethered to the pain of wrong, they can advance forward in righteousness, made right with God.

"I run in the path of your commands, for you have set my heart free" (Psalm 119:32).

Perhaps you've seen it. People who have chosen to forgive are more at peace and have a lighter heart because they are no longer carrying around the weight of the past. Their shoulders relax, and a smile replaces an angry scowl. By God's amazing grace and mercy, they are never the same.

What is binding you—bitterness, anger, resentment, or offense? Perhaps it's time to release your vice-grip hold and forgive. Give God your thirst, your ache, and your needs. As you choose to forgive and release, you will find freedom and peace.

It is always darkest before the dawn. But remember, daylight is coming, and so is your breakthrough.

PRAYER (WHEN YOU NEED TO *FORGIVE YOURSELF*)

Lord, I acknowledge that I have done things wrong and I am sorry. Please forgive me for my foolishness, ignorance, willful disobedience, and selfish ways. I don't want to live apart from You; I want to be near the One who loves me most, not far from Him. Would You please make me whole again? Wash over me as I release and let go. Thank You for Your unconditional love and healing. Thank You that Your mercies are new every morning. In Jesus' name, Amen.

PRAYER (WHEN YOU NEED TO *FORGIVE OTHERS*)

Lord, I come before You and I thank You that You know all things. You know what happened in this relationship. Right now I bring before You [say the person's name] and all the hurt and pain he (or she) has caused me. In my own strength I cannot let go, but I ask for the power of the Holy Spirit to help me forgive. Blow a fresh wind in my life and release the resentment, bitterness, and feelings of offense. Help me to forgive because You have forgiven me. I ask for courage, strength, and Your mighty power. In Jesus' name, Amen.

LIGHT FOR THE JOURNEY

If we confess our sins, he is faithful and just and will forgive us our sins and purify us from all unrighteousness. (I John 1:9)

Bear with each other and forgive whatever grievances you may have against one another. Forgive as the Lord forgave you. (Colossians 3:13)

Do not say, "I'll pay you back for this wrong!" Wait for the Lord, and he will deliver you. (Proverbs 20:22)

Do not be overcome by evil, but overcome evil with good. (Romans 12:21)

I run in the path of your commands, for you have set my heart free. (Psalm 119:32)

ILLUMINATION

1. What is forgiveness?

2. Why does God want us to forgive others?

3. Is there a difference between forgiveness and reconciliation?

4. Are there areas in your own life that need forgiving?

5. Are you aware of any childhood issues, trauma, or pain that is surfacing as you deal with this current heart pain? Whom do you need to forgive from past offenses?

6. Are there things that you need to forgive the person for with whom you just ended your relationship?

Part 3:
Dawn

Before
7 Sunrise:
Learning to
Wait Well

The night is nearly over; the day is almost here.
—Romans 13:12

I wait for the Lord, my soul waits,
and in his word I put my hope.
—Psalm 130:5

Early dawn, and it's just before sunrise. No longer night, but not yet day, this in-between time signals a significant shift. With darkness ending and day on the horizon, you begin to transition to a whole new frame of mind: waking up and walking on.

Your heart is in a time of transition, too. You've made it through the hardest part, and now you are farther from darkness and closer to light—and to your new beginning. As the pain fades, you're closer to peace; as the heartache fades, you're closer to hope. Faith is outshining fear, and better days are coming.

But between your breakup and brighter days there is still more healing to come and more to learn. In these next chapters you will find yourself awakening to hope, restoring your confidence and self-esteem, waking up to the rest of your life, and learning how to make healthier choices in your next relationship.

In the meantime, how do you learn to wait—and wait well?

WE DON'T LIKE WAITING

Most of us don't like to wait. In fact, we live in a world that promotes an instant-minded culture through commercials, billboards, radio spots, and online ads. *Act now! Get what you want when you want it* is the message we are saturated with every day. You can microwave your food, or better yet drive through a fast-food place and get your breakfast, lunch, or dinner already made and ready to go. We can fill our cupboards with instant oatmeal or instant soup, but when we try to get instant heart-healing from a breakup, we wind up unfulfilled and still hungry for hope.

When things seem to take too long for our own liking, instant gratification replaces waiting, and we may take matters into our own hands. We try to make something happen. Waiting makes some people feel restless or uneasy; it's hard to accept delay. Maybe you're afraid that you're missing out on something. You may be tired of the lingering heartache and you think getting into another relationship right away will fill the void. You don't know what to do with the spaces in life—like the interim gap between the guy who just left and the next one to come into your life.

WHAT ARE YOU WAITING FOR?

It is a lesson you learn and relearn throughout your entire life: waiting. When you're a kid, you can't wait to grow up or graduate from school. Then, you want time to pass quickly as you wait to hear if you got the job you wanted. You wonder what the holdup is when you wait to find a boyfriend, wait for him to call or commit, and wait to get married.

Much of life seems to have a time lag—that is, when we expect things to happen in the length of time *we* think it should take. People who are married often wonder when they'll have kids, or when the kids will grow up. We hunger for the day we'll get a better paying job, or finally use our talents in work or ministry. We long to lose weight, change a bad habit, or finally take that dream vacation—and we want it to happen right away. Whether it's for a delayed flight, or for cookies to bake, we wait.

Often we wonder if it's a delay (it'll happen someday) or a denial (it's never going to happen). When will my heart stop hurting? When will I find peace and joy again? When is it my turn to be a bride instead of the eternal bridesmaid? When is it my turn for love?

We wait for guidance, direction, and for answers—or we don't—and pay the consequences.

CONSEQUENCES OF NOT WAITING ON GOD

If waiting is a given, then we must decide if we will wait on God and learn to wait well, or force things to happen on our own and downright disobey. Either way, we will deal with the results.

For instance, if you drive through a red stoplight, another car could careen through the intersection and hit you, harming you and wrecking your car. Or, if you start another romantic relationship without waiting on God's timing, you'll carry the unhealed pain with you and you won't be able to give and receive love in the most stable or emotionally healthy way possible. You may end up driving the other person away or crashing the next relationship because you are simply not ready.

There are consequences of not waiting on God.

Centuries ago a woman named Sarah took matters into her own hands and the world is still living with the consequences of her decision. Abraham (Abram), Sarah's husband, was called by God to be "a great nation" (Genesis 12:2) and was told his offspring would be like the stars in the heavens—uncountable (Genesis 15:5), but the couple was childless well into their old age. Nevertheless, Abraham believed God. Sarah had a harder time with it. The rest of the story plays out in Genesis 16 and 17.

Sarah (who was called Sarai at the time) wanted things to happen faster and in her own way, so she told her husband to sleep with her maidservant, Hagar, and build a family through her. Abram agreed, and months later Ishmael was born. But before the infant arrived, Sarai had a bad attitude and began to despise and mistreat surrogate-mom Hagar. So Hagar fled and ended up in the desert where an angel of the Lord found her and told her to go back. The angel told her that her descendents would be too numerous to count, and the boy should be named Ishmael, meaning "God hears." In addition, Hagar learned that this child "will be a wild donkey of a man; his hand will be against everyone and everyone's hand against him, and he will live in hostility toward all his brothers" (Genesis 16:12).

By now Abram is ninety-nine years old. God changes his name to Abraham ("father of many") and his wife's to Sarah, and

God confirms that they will both be very fruitful and blessed.

Finally, the child of the promise was born. In Genesis 21, we learn that the Lord did as He had said. "Sarah became pregnant and bore a son to Abraham in his old age, *at the very time God had promised* him. Abraham gave the name Isaac to the son Sarah bore him (vv. 21: 2–3, emphasis mine). The new mother continues, "God has brought me laughter, and everyone who hears about this will laugh with me" (v. 6).

God has good reasons for delays. We may not always understand what He is doing and why, but God wants us to obey His commands—not because He is a tough taskmaster, but to protect us and guide us. In learning obedience, we also learn wisdom.

Like the wisdom of keeping your hands off the cocoon of an emerging butterfly. While you may want to help, it is not wise to pry it open for the little creature. He needs to build strength as he exits his temporary shelter or he will die. Know when to keep your hands off and trust God's ways and timing for things to unfold.

HOW TO WAIT WELL

Have you ever noticed that often God is not in a hurry? In the Bible we see a number of examples like the story above, as Abraham and Sarah waited years for a child. Joseph, a young man sold by his own brothers, lived in slavery (and at times, prison) for thirteen years before he rose to a powerful position in Egypt. And Jacob labored for fourteen years before he was released from Laban, the man whom he had to work for in order to earn the right to marry the man's two daughters. He worked six more years for his flocks.

God doesn't seem to be in a hurry because He is not on our timetable, we are on His. Often we tend to be more focused on the *results*, rather than the *process* of getting there. While we may think nothing is happening in the waiting times God is preparing and positioning us for what is next.

The truth is God is God, and we will never fully know His reasons. But we can take comfort in the fact that He is good, loving, and faithful—and He is always at work, even in the dark, putting together the pieces of our lives for His good purposes.

During seasons of waiting in our lives we learn that:

Waiting is active. Waiting is more than just passing time; it is *not* doing nothing. The *work of waiting* is believing God. Not just believing *in* God, but believing *Him.* It's trusting and having faith that the One who delights us in giving will provide what is best for each of us. It's a proactive time, not a passive one. You will discover in this chapter what you can do as you wait.

THE *WORK OF WAITING* is believing God. Not just believing *in* God, but believing *Him.*

We wait on God, not man. Waiting on God, not on a man (or yourself) makes all the difference. God had good purposes, so your waiting is not in vain. You don't have to be afraid that God will forget. He knows your heart; He knows you want love, affection, and attention. You can be confident and stand strong when it's Him upon whom you wait. "My soul, wait in silence for God only, for my hope is from Him. He only is my rock and my salvation, my stronghold; I shall not be shaken" (Psalm 62:5–6 NASB).

So instead of focusing on what you think you want (a boyfriend, a husband—the gift), focus on the Giver of good things. We can wait knowing He will answer us, whether it's with a "yes," "no," or "wait." Psalm 38:15 says, "I wait for you, O Lord; you will answer, O Lord my God."

Waiting draws us closer to God. Enduring delay builds intimacy and a closer relationship with Him. Jerome Daley in *When God Waits* says, "God's greatest purpose in seasons of waiting is to draw you close to himself, to reveal the depth of his commitment to you, and to equip you for your destiny."[1] The psalmist says, "Find rest, O my soul, *in God alone;* my hope comes from him. He alone is my rock and my salvation; he is my fortress, I will not be shaken" (Psalm 62:5–6, emphasis mine).

As I read over my journal from years in the post-breakup darkness, I can see how much I've changed. I can see growth. In that waiting time God's love for *me*, not just His general love for mankind, became more apparent and intense; I experienced it on deeper levels than I could have ever imagined. I learned that in our weakness, God is strong, and His strength precedes victory.

One of the biggest lessons I learned in my waiting season was *total dependence on God*—not a little bit of dependence when I felt like it—but complete reliance. As 2 Corinthians 1:9 says, we learn "that we might not rely on ourselves but on God."

Total dependence on God means that we are not so full of pride to think we can do this life on our own. As your breakup begins to seem farther away and you find yourself feeling emotionally stronger, you may think you can do life on your own. *I'll take it from here, God,* you think, *I've got it covered.* Really? When we don't see anything happening, we may foolishly step out and try to make things happen on our own. We can be confident but not prideful, secure but not foolish.

Waiting is for a purpose. God uses the seemingly dead times in our lives to heal, replenish, and prepare our hearts for the next season in our lives. Think of your heart as a fallow field. Like the farmer who leaves his land crop-free for a season, your heart may feel barren or blank, but it's only for a time. Leaving the land empty replenishes the soil and replaces the nutrients so a better, healthier crop grows the next time. In the same way, your "in the meantime" can be a time to heal and replenish your own heartland and, in time, gather a better and healthier yield in how you handle relationships—and life.

> GOD USES the seemingly dead times in our lives to heal, replenish, and prepare our hearts for the next season in our lives.

God keeps perfect time. Things unfold "in the fullness of time," when He is ready, when circumstances are ready, or when we are ready. You can't tell a newborn baby to run a marathon and then be disappointed when he does not. It's not time yet. He has to grow up first, and gain strength and muscle. You can't order a closed rosebud to "open up now!" It simply will not happen. In time the graceful flower unfolds. A line in a poem I wrote called "A Time for Everything" reads, "To everything there's a time and an hour, for our lives to unfold and for roses to flower. There's a reason and purpose for every delay, and with patience and timing we'll get there someday." Deliverance will come, healing will come; trust God's timing. "He has made everything beautiful in its time" (Ecclesiastes 3:11).

Waiting is a time of healing, transformation, and preparation.

You do your part and God does His part. Instead of sitting on the couch eating chips, hoping the breakup blues will disappear and the Lord will drop Mr. Wonderful onto your front porch, you have things to do. The art of waiting well begins as you learn how to live *as you wait.*

As you wait, prepare. Romans 13:12 says, "The night is nearly over; the day is almost here. So let us put aside the deeds of darkness and put on the armor of light." What do you need to put aside? What do you need to put on?

First, we take off, or actually let God wash off, the sin in our lives. "Let us behave decently, as in the daytime, not in orgies and drunkenness, not in sexual immorality and debauchery, not in dissension and jealousy" (v. 13). Cleansed, we put on the character of Christ. "Rather, clothe yourselves with the Lord Jesus Christ, and do not think about how to gratify the desires of the sinful nature" (v. 14). Take off and put on. Be ready.

Sometimes we need to develop more of our inner life so we are ready for the next season God has for us. We spend an amazing amount of time on the outside of our bodies with clothes, hair, and makeup, but we also need to grow on the inside. For instance, how can you restore your eroded confidence and self-esteem? You'll find out in chapter 9. Or, what do you want to do differently in your next relationship? Read chapter 11.

Preparation to grow up on the inside begins as we first "grow down," much like the roots of a bamboo tree. For the first six years, an extensive root system is developed under the earth. If you stood there and looked at where the bamboo tree was planted, you'd think nothing was happening. Finally, in the seventh year, the bamboo plant shoots up eighty feet tall! But only with such a widespread root system could the tree have the support it needed for such explosive growth. Although it seemed like nothing was happening, God was at work preparing for growth.

As you wait, pray. You can never go wrong when you put

God first. Waiting is a time of realignment, to get first things first and line up your heart with God again.

You may think you are too busy and don't have time to pray. But think of it not as *spending* time in prayer, but *investing* time in prayer. Just as you invest your financial resources to get a return, you invest time in prayer and the return is greater than anything you could imagine. Answered prayer, yes, but more importantly a closer, more enjoyable relationship with God. E. M. Bounds once said, "The goal of prayer is the ear of God, a goal that can only be reached by patient and continued and continuous waiting upon Him, pouring out our heart to Him and permitting Him to speak to us. Only by so doing can we expect to know Him, and as we come to know Him better we shall spend more time in His presence and find that presence a constant and ever-increasing delight."[2]

God knows the desires of your heart, and He hears you when you cry out to Him. "Be joyful in hope, patient in affliction, faithful in prayer" (Romans 12:12). Pray on.

As you wait, have patience. "Be still before the Lord and wait patiently for him" (Psalm 37:7). You can't rush the healing process of a broken heart. You can't make a new relationship come to you any faster. How do we endure delay when we don't know how long it will take to get to our destination or even how to get there?

Life often has unexpected twists and turns, and we need patience—persistence and staying power. Thankfully, God gives us guidance to stay on the right track. Our job is to listen and obey Him.

On the western shore of Lake Michigan, along the Wisconsin coastline, is Harrington Beach. One sunny Saturday I decided to drive there which, according to the map, should have taken less than two hours from my home in Milwaukee. As I drove along, I could finally see the lake on my right and thought I'd be there shortly. But suddenly the highway turned inland and soon I was driving past farmland and bright red barns. *This can't possibly be the way*, I thought. *I want to go to the beach, yet I'm driving inland past farms!*

I stopped at a gas station and asked the attendant if this was the right way to get to the beach, and he assured me it was. While the road had twists and bends, it would eventually lead to my destination. *Hmmm.* I guess I just needed to follow his directions and wait for the right exit. I pressed on.

Finally, there was a sign that pointed to the correct road to lead me to the beach. I parked my car and walked through a short wooded path and down a few wooden stairs. As I descended, I looked up and saw the most amazing expanse of sand and water I'd ever seen at a midwestern beach. To my right and left, miles of sand beckoned me to walk. The waves crashed on the shore, sea gulls cawed, and a gentle breeze blew off the lake and cooled me.

God knew the entire time that I'd get to the beach, even as I drove on winding roads that seemed to be going in the opposite direction. He knew the way; I did not. And I learned a big lesson in trust and patience that day. Waiting means that we trust God is leading us, guiding and directing. We are enduring delay even when the journey doesn't look how *we* think it should.

As you wait, rest. Rest is healing to the body and to the soul. "Come with me by yourselves to a quiet place and get some rest" (Mark 6:31). Jesus said those words to His apostles and they apply to us as well.

Mark Buchanan, in *The Rest of God: Restoring Your Soul by Restoring Sabbath*, said that rest is as essential to our well-being as food and water. That gives me pause to think. Without food and water I will die. Without rest, I will die on the inside. Buchanan says, "We simply haven't taken time. We've not been still long enough, often enough, to know ourselves, our friends, our family. Our God. Indeed, the worst hallucination busyness conjures is the conviction that *I am* God. *All depends on me. How will the right things happen at the right time if I'm not pushing and pulling and watching and worrying?"*[3]

As you wait, choose joy. Is it really possible to have joy, when you feel anything but joyful? In James 1:2, we read, "Consider it pure joy, my brothers, whenever you face trials of many kinds." *What? Why?* The author continues with the reason, "Because you know that the testing of your faith develops perseverance. Perseverance must finish its work so that you may be mature and complete, not lacking anything" (vv. 1:3–4).

Despite your circumstances, man or no man in your life, you can choose to have joy. Happiness may come and go, but joy is much more stable. Because God is in control, you can have peace. Because you cast your cares on God, and don't carry them, you can fully rely on His strength. And then a lighter heart emerges. Things may not have changed, but you have. No matter what is or is not happening in your life right now, soak in God's joy.

One of the most beautiful passages in Scripture on choosing joy is found in Habakkuk 3:17–18:

> Though the fig tree does not bud and there are no grapes on the vines, though the olive crop fails and the fields produce no food, though there are no sheep in the pen and no cattle in the stalls, yet I will rejoice in the Lord, I will be joyful in God my Savior.

Here is my translation of Habakkuk 3:17–18 for singles:

> Though the relationship does not bud and there are no men on the phone, though the love connection fails and the man produces no ring, though there are no dates in my Daytimer and no guys at the door . . . yet I will rejoice in the Lord, I will be joyful in God; He will take care of me.

As you wait, trust God's timing. God is always at work. We need to have faith and believe that His timing is perfect and His ways are for our ultimate good. In the fullness of time, things happen. His clock is not slow, nor fast, but always on time. It never needs batteries or recharging, and it never stops. Often, though, it's a different pace than ours.

Second Peter 3:8–9 reads, "But do not forget this one thing, dear friends: With the Lord a day is like a thousand years, and a thousand years are like a day. The Lord is not slow in keeping his promise, as some understand slowness. He is patient with you, not wanting anyone to perish, but everyone to come to repentance." No matter what you are waiting on, God will be faithful to you. It may be a new relationship or marriage, or it may be something you never expected. Whatever God gives, it is a gift to be cherished.

For years my friend Laura Lea longed to be married, have children, and keep a home. She was a school teacher and didn't meet many men there. Most of the people in her church were married, so there were not many prospects there either. So she went on with her life, and trusted God. She spent time with family and friends, pursued the heart of God, and even went to Russia for a year to work in an orphanage.

When she was almost forty, one of Laura Lea's room mothers at school asked if she would be interested in meeting a man named Harry. The room mother had been praying for a husband for Laura. She'd felt a tug in her heart to get them to meet. So Laura Lea met Harry over dinner at a restaurant and, as Harry said to Laura Lea, it was "you had me from hello." They are now married and have two adorable twins.

As you wait, persevere. Keep on going in your heart-healing journey and don't quit. You will make it—even when you don't feel like it! Galatians 6:9 states, "Let us not become weary in doing good, for at the proper time we will reap a harvest if we do not give up."

To be sure, it's not always easy to keep on going. We get tired. We get discouraged, and we don't always see results. In the movie *Cast Away*, Tom Hanks's character, Chuck, is stranded alone on a deserted island and his only "friend" is a volleyball named Wilson that washed ashore one day. He's been there a long time, and he has no idea if anyone is ever going to come and rescue him.

Finally, four years later, a large piece of sturdy plastic comes in with the tide enabling him to build a raft. And, after many days at sea, Chuck is rescued by a passing barge. Once home, a friend asks him how he made it through those long, lonely days and Chuck says, "You just have to keep breathing because someday the tide's gonna come in—and you never know what the tide's gonna bring with it." Keep breathing, keep trusting God, and hold on to hope.

Whatever it is you are waiting for—for your heart to stop hurting, for a new relationship, for a better job, or for your long-held dreams to come true, press on. And take heart that all things really do work together for the good (Romans 8:28).

As you wait, live "now" and look ahead. Getting over a relationship with someone you truly cared about or loved can be hard—really hard. Sometimes you may let your thoughts linger in the past, or yearn for a time that no longer exists. You may obsess about a person who is no longer available and that can damage your self-esteem as well as prevent you from moving forward into your future—and into the life of someone who will love you with a real and lasting love in return.

It took Travis years to look forward with hope instead of looking back over his shoulder at the past. Getting over Hannah was the hardest thing he had ever done.

Travis and Hannah met at church and were good friends for two or three years before they started dating. They spent a lot of time together and even went on vacations with their children from previous marriages. Travis was love-struck and he would do anything for this woman—he used his handyman skills and fixed up her house, he watched her dog when she was out of town, and he had her kids over to his house when she needed a break. Of course, it was kind of him to do all of those things in a committed relationship. However, when they broke up, he continued to be there for her and she began to take advantage of the situation.

While Hannah only wanted a friendship, Travis still wanted to marry her and he found it excruciating to try and separate from this person with whom his life had been so enmeshed.

For the next few years they bounced between being off and being on again as a couple, but Travis still could not let go. Finally, he came to a point where he realized that he was doing all the giving and Hannah was doing all the taking, and he made a decision to move on. Travis wanted someone with whom love would be reciprocated and not one-sided. So he told her that he needed to cut off all contact with each other, at least for a time. It was the only way Travis could break free from her, heal, and move forward with his life.

So for a period of time there were no phone calls, texts, or e-mails. He blocked her from his Facebook and took down all the photos he had of her in his house. It was time. But it was also immensely difficult, like detoxing from a drug. Travis knew that eventually it would be okay; in time the cravings for her would fade.

God gave him the emotional strength to release what he'd held to so tightly for years. Instead of fixating on the past, he was facing forward—looking toward his future—toward sunrise. He was learning to live in the present and have hope for his new beginning. He took the initiative to develop new friendships and reconnect with people he knew from Bible studies and church.

Isaiah 43:18–19 reads, "Forget the former things; do not dwell on the past. See, I am doing a new thing! Now it springs up;

do you not perceive it? I am making a way in the desert and streams in the wasteland." Travis had no idea that something new and good was about to water his desert-dry heart and invigorate his life.

As we process the hurt and release the pain through the power of forgiveness, we can learn to live in the present. We can be okay with now and look forward with hope.

WAITING PURIFIES OUR HOPE FOR GOD

Waiting builds character, strengthens our dependence upon God, and draws us closer to Him. It protects us from harm and grows us up on the inside. Waiting is for a reason. "God lets us wait—not to punish us, not because he has forgotten us, but because our waiting is the crucible he uses to purify our hope for him," says Dan Allender.[4]

Morning will be here soon, your better and brighter days. The first streams of sunlight are beginning to appear in the eastern sky—and so are the first rays of hope.

PRAYER

Lord, it's hard to live in the meantime and sometimes it's really hard to wait. I want the pain to go away. I want to feel better and find someone new. And yet, Your priorities are different than mine. Help me to learn to wait well for what is ahead for me. Help me to remember that You keep perfect time. As I wait on You, Lord, show me how to prepare. Teach me to pray, have patience, and persevere. Fill me with Your joy as I rest and trust in You. In Jesus' name, Amen.

LIGHT FOR THE JOURNEY

I wait for you, O Lord; you will answer, O Lord my God. (Psalm 38:15).

I waited patiently for the Lord; and He inclined to me and heard my cry. (Psalm 40:1 NASB)

I wait for the Lord, my soul waits, and in his word I put my hope. (Psalm 130:5)

ILLUMINATION

1. What does it mean to "wait well"?

2. What helps you to *not* take matters into your own hands and wait on God?

3. What is the hardest part of waiting for you?

4. What are some important lessons you have learned so far? Pray and ask God to reveal to you what is keeping you linked to the past.

8

First Light:
Awakening Hope

Even if you are not ready for day
it cannot always be night.
—Gwendolyn Brooks, poet

Where I live in the foothills of the Rocky Mountains, sunrise can be spectacular. The fingers of early morning crawl across the eastern plains, gradually illuminating the city skyline, and increasing in brightness to reveal—like footlights on a stage—the splendor of the majestic snowcapped Pikes Peak. You can almost hear the Director signaling His creation, "Cue the morning; let a new day begin!"

The sun bids the darkness farewell, and the earth awakens. It is a fresh start in your Heart Land as well, as your residual breakup pain fades and hope wakes up. Heartache is turning to healing.

At the break of day, birds chirp cheerily, the alarm rings (not so cheerily), and sunlight streams through your bedroom window announcing the arrival of morning. The aroma of fresh coffee or hot tea beckons.

But for some people it's hard to get up and get going. In this half-asleep-but-not-yet-awake stage, they rouse and stir a bit, yawn and stretch, and then roll over and go back to sleep. They don't want to get up yet. It's too early, or they're too tired, or they simply have no motivation to get out of bed. Perhaps they want to hold on to the last vestiges of night and linger in the darkness.

Others, bless their "I'm-a-morning-person" hearts, are exuberant at the crack of dawn. They spring from slumber to waking with the lively energy of Winnie the Pooh's friend Tigger, full of bounce and ready to start the day.

Either way, getting out of bed is a choice. Just as having hope is a choice. You can choose to stay asleep in the darkness of bitterness, resentment, and hopelessness. With the curtains closed tightly and no light penetrating your heart, you wallow and mope, and keep moping.

Or instead, you could choose to follow the way of hope, and

keep hoping, choosing to move forward into the full light of day—into the fullness of the abundant life of greater peace, joy, and wholeness. The outcome of each path is entirely different.

NOT READY FOR DAYLIGHT

If you are not yet ready for day, you may hesitate moving forward for many reasons. Perhaps your mind keeps wandering back to Memory Lane when things were good and life was happier. Or, you stress and obsess that maybe he will reconsider. Perhaps you feel like you've been emotionally sleepwalking, going through the motions of life, but you're not fully aware or awake on the inside. For whatever reason, hope is stirring, but it's thwarted.

The problem is when you've been hurt and your hopes have been dashed, it can be hard to move forward and have hope—not only in a new relationship but in life. Especially if you've had many breakups, you get tired of the repeated discouragement. It hurts. It's hard. And you never want to go through it again. So you put hope to sleep in your life because you don't want to be disappointed again. You are stuck in your story.

It's time to get up.

Of course, adjusting to the light can be difficult at first. Often when I open my blinds in the morning and brightness fills the room, I have to squint at first. It takes time for your eyes to adjust, just as it takes time for your heart to adjust from the darkness of despair to the light of hope.

MENDING POINTS

Is there a specific point when night becomes day, or when hurt turns to hope? If there is a "breaking point," is there also a "mending point"?

Dawn turns to day gradually, not suddenly. In the same way, heart-healing from a breakup is a process. It's a series of actions and choices. Healing takes time, and massive amounts of God's truth being poured into you to combat the feelings and lies that say it will always hurt, it will never get better, or you will never find love again.

My friend Ken once remarked to me about the changing of the seasons, and how you don't always notice an exact point when the transition occurred. It is gradual, and alights on you when you least expect it. But one day you notice that the lifeless, cement-gray world you've known for months has been transformed into blue skies and blossoms. *When did that happen?* You see the effects of it, but you may not be aware of the exact moment it changed.

While there may not be a specific "mending point" in your heart-healing, it may be a series of moments or progression of turning points. Moments like hearing the comforting words of a friend, or reading an insightful quote from a book, or learning a lesson from nature, or the unexpected warmth of God's presence wrapped around you, and you awaken to the realization that one day everything will be okay. And you are well on your way to day—and hope.

Still, I've often wished the path from hurt to hope could be easier, clearer. When you decide to take a trip and pull out a map, you can locate a specific starting point and ending point. Plus, you have a destination, and when you get there you know you've arrived.

In breakup world, there is no perfect map. There is a path that each of us follows. There are good ideas and guidelines—and certainly God's Word—but *how* that combination works to get you to a better place is different for each of us. There is no wooden sign that tells you the exact moment you are exiting pain and entering peace, as in "You are now leaving the land of loss" or "Welcome to the land of new beginnings."

You have to walk in faith.

And you must choose which road to walk.

THE HEART'S "GREAT AWAKENING"

Time has passed since your breakup. Whether it's been weeks, months, or years, eventually your slumbering self wakes up and the light of God's truth brings greater revelation. You have more awareness, insight, and clarity about your pain and the relationship ending. You've come a long way in your healing journey.

And now you stand at a crossroads. There is a fork in the road, and before you are two paths. One is the way of hope—Hope Road. The other is the path of hopelessness—Despair Drive. It is a defining moment, to have hope or not. Which road will you take?

Despair Drive follows the trail of bleakness. You just want to give up. You don't want to deal with this "getting over a breakup" stuff any longer; you want to stay asleep and succumb to the darkness of disappointment. It's too difficult, and it's taking too long.

You show up for work or for lunch with friends, but a part of you is not really there. You've kind of checked out; the lights are on but no one's home. You've been rejected and you can't seem to get over it. Somehow you think a broken heart is incurable.

But beware: walking down Despair Drive is dangerous. And not making a decision about which path to take is in itself a decision. It's understandable to have a heavy heart after a breakup, but don't "lose heart." Resignation to hopelessness can lead to isolation, alienation, and further misery. You may even often miss out on support, love, and friendship, the very things you need.

Despair Drive or Hope Road? It's your choice. God has called you "out of darkness into his wonderful light" (1 Peter 2:9). How will you answer?

THE WAY OF HOPE

Choosing Hope Road is a "one prayer at a time; one choice at a time" path that leads to a more whole and healthier attitude and life. You start out by taking your first steps. As you walk on, roadblocks may come your way, but you navigate obstacles with God's help. As you choose to follow Hope Road, and keep following, you learn to listen and obey God's words and take action.

> CHOOSING HOPE ROAD
> is a "one prayer at a time;
> one choice at a time" path
> that leads to a more whole
> and healthier attitude and life.

You also have a sense of destination that you're on your way to a better place—the abundant life—the rich, full life Jesus promised us in John 10:10: "I have come that they may have life, and have it to the full." The abundant life is not about accumulating stuff, it's about being spiritually full, bursting with the goodness of God in your life, not bleak or empty. It's learning to walk in victory, not being a victim to circumstances, and finding satisfaction and joyful confidence because you know who you are and whose you are.

FIRST STEPS

It takes courage to step out on a new path. Whether you begin hesitantly or with a let's-have-an-adventure excitement, the important thing is that you begin—and keep choosing hope. You seek the Lord and listen for His guidance. "Whether you turn to the right or to the left, your ears will hear a voice behind you, saying, 'This is the way; walk in it'" (Isaiah 30:21).

By taking one step, and then another and another, you leave the old place of brokenness and rubble, fraught with complications and unanswered questions. Even when the future is unclear and it feels like a primordial haze hangs over your heart, walk on. Because like the early morning low cloudiness in San Francisco, eventually the fog will lift and clarity will come. Your blue sky days of joy will return. Have hope.

ROADBLOCKS TO HOPE

Be assured, though, that walking with hope is not like being in a Disney cartoon where bluebirds carrying colorful ribbons lead the way and happy chipmunks wave as you skip down the lane and daisies bloom instantly at your feet. As you walk down Hope Road, you may have obstacles or roadblocks. You may not be able to see the way ahead or you may feel lost. What are some things that can block hope?

Not knowing the difference between false hope and true hope. After a relationship ends, you may hope the one you cared about will come back. "False hope" is when you expect him to return when it's highly unlikely or even impossible that he will. Because you want it to happen so badly, you may deny the reality that he is already in another relationship, that he's married, or that—for whatever reason—he is going in another direction without you. You can, however, be optimistic that things will get better in your life and that God has good things for you down the road.

Romance novels or movies can also lead to a sense of false hope. While I enjoy watching a good romantic comedy once in a while, we need to remember to enjoy the show for the purpose of entertainment not for the reality factor.

In the movies, the leading couple often seems supermagnetically drawn to each other; they inescapably *must* be together, because they are "soul mates." Each is the only one who will ever satisfy the other. With this particular person, life is bliss; without them, life is bankrupt. The guy pursues intensely and despite an inordinate number of obstacles, he eventually gets the girl and they live happily ever after. Or so we are led to believe. The credits roll and you never see the rest of the story. *Now what?*

In real life, couples have everyday struggles that go along with being in a dating relationship or marriage. In real life, men don't always pursue, they can evade asking you out or avoid a real commitment for years. Also, many women have expectations that a man will know exactly what to say and do to make their heart melt, and when he does not, they are baffled. The thing is, in real life, men don't have a script to follow!

Keep in mind that you are wired with a longing for love; it is good to want to be pursued and to desire someone with whom you can spend the rest of your life. While your heart may ache to be the leading lady in your favorite chick flick, God wants to author a love story for you that is genuine, godly, and divinely designed for you. That is something for which you can pray and hope.

False hope is like being a Pollyanna—optimistic, yet blind to reality. It is wishful thinking or vain imaginations. Real hope, biblical hope, is different.

Biblical hope is confident trust in the reliability of God's promises. It is solid and strong because it is based upon God's words in the Bible. "For everything that was written in the past was written to teach us, so that through endurance and the encouragement of the Scriptures we might have hope" (Romans 15:4).

Hope presses on and looks ahead. "Brothers, I do not consider myself yet to have taken hold of it. But one thing I do: Forgetting what is behind and straining toward what is ahead, I press on toward the goal to win the prize for which God has called me heavenward in Christ Jesus" (Philippians 3:13–14).

Day or night, we can ask God to show us what to do, to guide our path so we can look forward with trust, not trepidation. "Show me your ways, O Lord, teach me your paths; guide me in your truth and teach me, for you are God my Savior, and my hope is in you *all day long*" (Psalm 25:4–5, emphasis mine).

> "HOPING IS NOT dreaming. It is not spinning an illusion or fantasy to protect us from our boredom or our pain. It means a confident, alert expectation that God will do what he said he will do. It is a willingness to let God do it his way and in his time."
> —Eugene Peterson

When Hope Road seems to zigzag and you cannot see the way ahead, Hebrews 10:23 encourages you to press on with confidence and perseverance: "Let us hold unswervingly to the hope we profess, for he who promised is faithful."

Finally, biblical hope believes that God will give good things. He protects and He provides as He sees best. "For the Lord God is a sun and shield; the Lord bestows favor and honor; *no good thing does he withhold* from those whose walk is blameless" (Psalm 84:11, emphasis mine).

Eugene Peterson said, "Hoping is not dreaming. It is not spinning an illusion or fantasy to protect us from our boredom or our pain. It means a confident, alert expectation that God will do what he said he will do. It is a willingness to let God do it his way and in his time."[1]

Fear and doubt. Another roadblock to hope is the double-punch combination of fear and doubt. It's important to know that even when you are hopeful it doesn't mean you will never again give in to fear or doubt. God knows that we're human; He created us! So He asks us to "cast our cares" and not reel them back in. Psalm 55:22 reads, "Cast your cares on the Lord and he will sustain you; he will never let the righteous fall."

Gently, the Lord takes your hand, knowing your fears and failures, and leads you down Hope Road. You walk together. "For I am the Lord, your God, who takes hold of your right hand and says to you, Do not fear; I will help you" (Isaiah 41:13).

You're unclear on what you're hoping for. One day I was standing in the middle of the grocery store, surrounded by thousands of cans, boxes, and fresh food items, yet I had no idea what I wanted. I could have anything, yet nothing appealed to me. What was I hungry for? As I thought about it, I came to realize that I wasn't hungry at all, I was thirsty. I was confusing hunger with thirst.

Sometimes we confuse hunger with thirst in matters of the heart. You may think you want a new relationship right now, one that will fill your heart's hunger for love while you are getting over the pain of the past, but you're really thirsty. The bone-dry ache inside you is actually panting for the love of God to quench, refresh, and fill you up.

First address your thirst. Get filled up on the inside with the living water that satisfies, then the Lord will attend to your heart hunger. "Delight yourself in the Lord and he will give you the desires of your heart" (Psalm 37:4).

As you walk the road of hope, it's important that you know what you are hoping for—what it is you want. You may hope the sting of rejection will end and you'll feel better sooner than later. You may look forward to the day when you walk arm in arm with someone special, or you don't have to sit alone at church. You hope that the next guy you're with will light up your world when he smiles, and that he'll be this amazing combination of someone who can talk easily about spiritual things but who is also fun and playful—someone who really understands you.

Whether it's a new boyfriend, an incredible husband, or someone who notices you, it's not wrong to hope for lasting love. What do you hope for? Are you willing to put God first, and allow Him to give you the desires of your heart in His ways and in His timing?

I had hoped my relationship with Brian would have turned out differently. I was twentysomething when I met him at a birthday party for one of my closest friends. I had only planned on going to the party for an hour; I ended up staying twelve.

Just as I had been ready to leave, my friend told me that someone had been noticing me and excitedly introduced me to Brian. He was in town from southern California visiting his sister who lived in the same apartment complex as my friend.

We talked and laughed for hours. Even after the party ended, we sat in his car talking until the first rays of sunrise peered over his dashboard. The next day he asked me to have dinner with him, so we went to a waterfront restaurant and talked well into the night. He was so easy to be with, and I felt comfortable and good in his company.

We met again for breakfast before he left two days later, and over the next few months we kept in touch. He wrote postcards from the ocean community where he lived, and we made plans for me to visit. When I arrived, we picked up right where we had left off five months earlier. I met his friends, we went to the beach, and we connected. It all seemed so right until it was apparent that it was all so wrong.

Brian was great, except for the fact that he was not a believer. I don't think he followed any religion, and it was becoming a rift between us. I knew that dating and marrying someone who shared my Christian beliefs was a priority, but at the time I was letting my feelings lead instead of my convictions. I just needed the courage to end it. Instead, Brian did. He could sense that my faith would always be first. At the end of the visit, we said good-bye at a restaurant on an ocean pier and it was over.

I really liked Brian. But I loved God more.

Misplaced hope. When something is in the wrong place or lost, it is often called "misplaced." When we hope in a person or a thing to fulfill us instead of God, then our hope is misplaced. Our thought life can get hijacked on the highway of hope when we succumb to erroneous "if only" thinking: *If only I had a boyfriend, then I'd be happy. When I get married, then I will never be lonely again. Once we have a baby, things will get better. If only I could get that job, then I'd really get ahead.*

My friend Paul, a doctor, was single for years before he married at age thirty-nine. "When I was single and wanted to be married, I struggled with thinking that God didn't love me or I'd be married," he told me. As a strong believer, Paul knew that the Evil One tries to skew our perspective and keep us from trusting God. "Satan wants to deceive us into thinking God doesn't love us or want the best for us," he said.

But his perspective changed and his hope was redirected when he read Romans 5:8, "But God demonstrates his own love for us in this: While we were still sinners, Christ died for us." Paul knew that God loved him, but reading it again helped him to remember that God loved *him*. And, God loves each of us, no matter if we get what we want or not.

Paul was encouraged. He said, "God doesn't demonstrate His love toward us in that we will be married. He demonstrates His love in all He has done for us in the past, and all he continues to do for us every single day." Paul recognized that while He had the *desire* to be married, he needed to change his *focus*. Instead of looking only at his yearning for a wife, he began to think about and do more "kingdom things," eternal things, especially worship. He started by listing some of the attributes of God, praying, "I praise You God that You are loving, merciful, just, compassionate . . ." and put his focus on God first.

> WHETHER YOU are single or married, hard times will come, and becoming equipped with a hope-filled heart is essential no matter what your marital status.

Whether you are single or married, hard times will come, and becoming equipped with a hope-filled heart is essential no matter what your marital status. Paul and his wife, Tammy, both walked the intensely difficult road of dealing with infertility for more than five years. They longed for a baby, but after multiple tests, surgeries, and doctors reports, they learned that their chances of getting pregnant were slim to none.

As she persevered in prayer, Tammy learned to find hope and joy in today—not tomorrow or yesterday. "I would pray every day, 'Lord, I want just as much joy now as I will have when my "promise" comes,'" said Tammy. She discovered that God gave her joy in her relationship with Him and in many other things during that time.

Even though it was a season of longing and lack, Tammy also

asked God to "do what He couldn't do at any other time." In other words, she wanted *everything* God had to give her, to teach her in that season of life. She had hope that the bleakness of winter would not last forever, and in time their springtime finally arrived. Today this couple is blessed with a beautiful and healthy baby girl, Elliana Joy, and they appreciate this child so much more because of the struggle and God's faithfulness to them.

When nothing seems to be happening, when you are tired of trying to make things work out on your own, when you cannot see ahead and you think things are taking entirely too long, hold on to hope. The cadence of Christ is often unlike your own pace, but God is still at work, always at work, in your life. "Hope has its own rhythm," said Larry Crabb in *Shattered Dreams.* "We cannot rush it. The water of life will find its way down the mountain to fill the lake from which we can drink."[2]

Knowing God is with us every step of the way enables us to continue and not give in to despair. We walk on with hope, with Jesus. "I'm staying on your trail [Lord]; I'm putting one foot in front of the other. I'm not giving up" (Psalm 17:5 THE MESSAGE).

OVERCOMING OBSTACLES TO HOPE

If hope is asleep in your life, how can you overcome the obstacles? How does hope awaken?

Hope awakens because God arises. Despite the difficulties, you have the strength to wake up and walk on because God arises first. He lifts you up; He helps you to soar above your adversity. Psalm 68:1 says, "May God arise, may his enemies be scattered; may his foes flee before him."

At first you may think, *I don't have any enemies.* And then it dawns on you that you do have opponents on the road to hope and healing. In addition to the Evil One, our main adversary, difficulties like worry, fear, doubt, rejection, obsession, anxiety are "enemies" as well. They can come at you with the force of an opposing army, and much of this book is dedicated to helping you overcome blockages that prevent you from living in the peace and promises of God.

Hope rises above angst, dread, and unrequited passion—above feelings. We can march confidently into the future because "we live by faith, not by sight" (2 Corinthians 5:7).

Author Judith Couchman says, "Without hope, people perish. With God's hope, they believe beyond themselves. Hope isn't something we muscle up. Rather, it's the outflow of God's love in human hearts. . . ."[3]

Hope awakens from unconditional love. The total and absolute love of God and the supportive love of family and friends changes us from the inside out. On this path of heart-healing know that you are loved, cared for, and never alone. "His love endures forever" (Psalm 136).

Hope awakens because God is our anchor. When a boat is anchored, it doesn't drift away. When your life is anchored in Christ and the winds of adversity blow, your life won't drift aimlessly into the waters of hopelessness, discouragement, or false teachings. Constant and unwavering, the God who stays is your anchor of hope. "We have this hope as an anchor for the soul, firm and secure" (Hebrews 6:19).

I asked my dad recently what gave him hope, and he told me the words of Jesus, "I am with you always" (quoted in Matthew 28:20). God's presence and his lifelong belief in the Father, Son, and Holy Spirit—they are my dad's steady anchor. He continued, "It's about spiritual training . . ." and I was reminded how my instruction in Christian basics as a child first formed my faith and held me steady, anchored to Jesus, during tumultuous times.

Hope awakens from God's Word. "For everything that was written in the past was written to teach us, so that through endurance and the encouragement of the Scriptures we might have hope" (Romans 15:4). The Scriptures, the Holy Bible, God's Word are all names for the central text of our faith. What a blessing it is to have these words of hope in our own language. They are words that Jesus spoke, words that healed the blind, lame, and sick, and words that will heal your pain-weary heart. "Why are you downcast, O my soul? Why so disturbed within me? Put your hope in God, for I will yet praise him, my Savior and my God" (Psalm 42:5).

Hope awakens to God's sovereignty. Perhaps one of the biggest lessons I've learned from enduring breakups is that my love life is not entirely up to me. God directs and redirects. He is sovereign; He is in control. "The mind of man plans his way, but the Lord directs his steps" (Proverbs 16:9 NASB).

It was becoming apparent to me that God was redirecting my life as a long-term relationship was fading. I was driving this man to the airport to drop him off for a trip. Although I thought we were really good together, it was obvious his heart was going in another direction.

As we drove, words unexpectedly came tumbling out of my mouth that weren't in my heart seconds earlier, "I don't think this breakup is about you or me." He looked at me quizzically.

I continued, "I think God is redirecting our lives, and He has a different life path for each of us. It just doesn't include us being together."

I knew it was the Lord leading me to speak those words because it surely wasn't my idea. While it felt odd to say it, somehow I knew in my heart it was true. And though I cared deeply for this man, I knew at that moment that we would not serve God together in marriage; we would serve Him apart.

As hard as it was to separate from him, I came to realize that our breakup was not so much about this man rejecting *me*, it was about God redirecting our lives.

We can make our plans, but the Lord promotes or prevents; He advances or denies. When love (or like) ends, it is only because the One who loves you most is moving you into a new beginning.

> THE GOD of all hope
> is consistently faithful
> and always at work
> behind the scenes.

FRESH HOPE DELIVERED DAILY

Every morning the sun rises; every day the Lord delivers fresh hope. Despite the discouragement and difficulties, you can look back at all God has done in the past in other areas of your life— how He's kept His promises and has been faithful to keep His word—and you can look forward to good things to come in the future. A new sunrise, and bright hope.

> Yet this I call to mind and therefore I have hope:
> Because of the Lord's great love we are not consumed, for his compassions never fail. They are new every morning; great is your faithfulness. (Lamentations 3:21–23)

DESTINATION: ABUNDANT LIFE

Stay on Hope Road and keep on walking. God has good purposes for you, and you may be surprised at what is ahead. "'For I know the plans I have for you,' declares the Lord, 'plans to prosper you and not to harm you, plans to give you hope and a future. Then you will call upon me and come and pray to me, and I will listen to you. You will seek me and find me when you seek me with all your heart'" (Jeremiah 29:11–13).

Hope is confident expectation that you will receive what you hope for, that a desire will come to pass. If you planted dahlia seeds in your garden, you would hope that one day the brightly colored flowers would spring up. As you covered the seeds with dark brown soil, you'd be confident that, in time, there would be growth even though you do not yet see results. Romans 8:24–25 says, "Hope that is seen is no hope at all. Who hopes for what he already has? But if we hope for what we do not yet have, we wait for it patiently."

We long for the day when all we hope for will be seen, and we can echo the words of the prophet Isaiah, "O Lord, you are my God; I will exalt you and praise your name, for in perfect faithfulness you have done marvelous things, things planned long ago" (Isaiah 25:1).

Until then, we wait with joyful and expectant hope, knowing that the God of all hope is consistently faithful and always at work behind the scenes.

BEHIND THE SCENES

Imagine you are seated in a grand theater waiting for a play to begin. But you are months early. As you sit alone in the theater, you think that nothing is happening because all you can see are empty seats and a closed curtain.

You cannot see the flurry of activity on the other side of the curtain. Behind the scenes actors are learning their lines, builders are creating sets, and costume designers are rushing to fashion just the right outfits for the performers.

Then one day, finally, it is time. The orchestra begins, the house lights dim, the curtains open, and the show begins.

Just because you cannot see, it doesn't mean nothing is happening. God is always at work—night and day, dusk and dawn. One day the curtains will part in your life, and you will see what God has been doing behind the scenes for you.

There is life after loss, joy after sorrow, and peace after pain.

Believe, even when you cannot see. "Blessed is she who has believed that what the Lord has said to her will be accomplished!" (Luke 1:45).

Hope is stirring. My prayer for you is that you would look forward with faith, and "know the hope" to which God has called you. With the rising sunlight, you will be better able to see.

I pray also that the eyes of your heart may be enlightened in order *that you may know the hope* to which he has called you, the riches of his glorious inheritance in the saints, and his incomparably great power for us who believe. (Ephesians 1:18–19, emphasis mine)

PRAYER

Lord, I need more hope in my life. I need more of You. I feel like I've been asleep, dead to the world and dead in my heart. Would You help me to let go of discouragement and depression in my life? I don't want to be like this anymore. I want to run to the feet of Jesus and find comfort, strength, and deeper character. Thank You for showing me that, in Your loving sovereignty, You direct and redirect my life. You have new things for me, good things. Help me to look forward with faith. Enlighten my eyes and my heart to see Your faithfulness—all You have done for me in the past, and all You are doing now on this road from breakup to better days. I put my trust in You. In Jesus' name, Amen.

LIGHT FOR THE JOURNEY

Where morning dawns and evening fades you call forth songs of joy. (Psalm 65:8)

But blessed are those who trust in the Lord and have made the Lord their hope and confidence. (Jeremiah 17:7 NLT)

May the God of hope fill you with all joy and peace as you trust in him, so that you may overflow with hope by the power of the Holy Spirit. (Romans 15:13)

On him we have set our hope that he will continue to deliver us. (2 Corinthians 1:10)

ILLUMINATION

1. Have you ever felt like you have been emotionally "sleep-walking" through life (i.e., being physically present but not showing up emotionally or engaging with others)?

2. Have you had any specific "turning points" on your road of breakup recovery? List something that happened that caused you to know it was going to be okay.

3. What are some reasons to choose Hope Road (hope) over Despair Drive (hopelessness)?

4. How is "false hope" different from true or biblical hope?

5. What are one or two Bible verses that are meaningful to you in this chapter?

Illumination:

9 Restoring Confidence and Self-Esteem

This is who you are, your identity,
LOVED BY GOD.
—Eugene Peterson

It all began with a single spark. The summer of 2002 had been one of the driest in decades and our state was enduring a drought when the largest forest fire in Colorado's history, the Hayman Fire, started in the Pike National Forest. From where I live, just over an hour's drive away, you could see residual smoke blowing over the mountains. Some days you could see pieces of white ash floating from the sky onto the city streets, cars, and people. Sadly, this inferno was ignited when a forest service officer was burning a letter from her estranged husband. The devastation was enormous; it caused thousands of people to evacuate their homes, totally destroyed over a hundred of them, and burned about 138,000 acres.

Months later, some friends and I flew over the burn scar area in a small plane and we could see for miles the desolate landscape and the remnants of black charred tree limbs. But even though the flames were out, forestry officials had a significant new problem on their hands—erosion.

The intense heat of the fire had destroyed the protective layer of groundcover over the soil (like plants, grass, shrubs, and even litter). With the topsoil washed away because of the erosion, tree roots were exposed and unprotected, and the plant life was vulnerable to damage and depleted of nutrients.

Recovery efforts began quickly to help restore the immediate harm to the environment and to prevent further erosion when the high winds would come and rainwater would run down the mountain slopes. Forest officials reseeded the area with grasses so the plant roots could stabilize the soil. They erected log barriers to prevent rainwater run off and restored essential drainage areas.

Just as a forest fire can lead to erosion of soil, the fire of harsh words, negative comments, or repeated rejection can begin to wear away at your self-esteem.

EMOTIONAL EROSION

Emotional erosion often begins in childhood; even as a child's image of herself is being formed it may also be torn down. Parents are supposed to protect, provide for, and praise children, guiding and helping them grow into healthy, whole adults. But when a child is put down, belittled, and constantly criticized— wounded with words— she doesn't feel safe, accepted, or wanted. If she is continually ignored or abandoned, even by parents who are physically present but emotionally unavailable, she may feel depleted at an early age. Void of the nutrients of love, care, and consistency children need most, a little girl may have no idea how valuable and precious she really is.

Over the years the landscape of her heart begins to change. The constant dripping of another's anger or ridicule, or living unnoticed begins to form a rut, then a gully, and the wearing away of self-esteem continues. As an adult she feels hollow, disconnected, and she may have tendencies toward perfectionism, people pleasing, or depression.

She feels like she is never "enough"—good enough, thin enough, pretty enough, smart enough, or whatever enough—for anyone to love her consistently and well. Guys come and go, and breakup after breakup over the years reinforces her feelings of being unloved, unworthy, or less than. Hope withers and self-esteems sags. Like the pinkish-purple ice plants that close up at night, a wounded woman hides her beauty and her true self.

OTHER CAUSES OF EMOTIONAL EROSION

What are some other things that cause emotional erosion and seem to wash away self-esteem and confidence after a breakup?

Rejection. Rejection is one of the biggest self-esteem crushers, whether it's from the crumbling of a long-term relationship or an I-don't-think-so brush-off after a few dates. You hope, you wonder, and you take a risk with someone. Then you break-up and feel like you've lost again. It can do a number on your self-esteem, and you wonder how you'll muster the confidence and courage to start all over with someone new.

After getting my heart crushed a few years ago, I took a break from dating for a number of months. Then I met someone whom I'll call Coffee Guy. I assumed we were just friends because we only saw each other every few weeks, but he seemed consistent. We sat together at church on Sundays, we went to events, and drank a lot of coffee.

After almost a year of "hanging out," I confronted Coffee Guy one afternoon. "So, do you ever see us being more than just friends?" I asked. He looked right at me and calmly said, "No. I don't." We exchanged a few more words, and that was it. He moved on.

In hindsight I can see that we should've had a DTR (define-the-relationship) talk much sooner, but I was always waiting for him to bring it up. He never did. Even though we were just hanging out, I felt let down and frustrated. *Why do guys do this? They act like they like you, but they never get it into gear!* Even though it wasn't a big deal breakup, it was one more rejection wearing away at my self-esteem.

Distorted perception of yourself. A distorted perspective of something is fuzzy and imprecise, and often untrue. When I was in eighth grade I got my first pair of eyeglasses. I remember looking out the window at the trees and noticing how clearly I could distinguish each individual leaf. With the clarity the glasses provided, blurry green blobs on a stick transformed into majestic maple and oak trees.

Sometimes we don't see ourselves clearly either. The lenses through which we've been viewing our lives have been distorted by the constant criticism of a parent, the degrading comments from kids at school, or by the downright mean way someone has treated you.

Jud Wilhite said, "Distorted images are not only shaping your perspective but are also hindering your possibilities." In *Eyes Wide Open*, he explains, "If you see yourself as insignificant long enough, you'll start to act accordingly. If you see yourself as ugly or worthless, it will affect how you relate to your family and friends, your God and your world. Rather than grow and change as you could, you'll be tempted to give in or give up or stay in a holding pattern of self-destructive behavior. Rather than make your own unique contribution in the world, you may pull back and settle for mediocrity. But this is not the real you."[1]

We need God's better-than-20/20-vision to gain a clearer vision of who we really are, to come out of hiding, to be courageous, and to see ourselves as He sees us. "The real you emerges as you see differently, *biblically*. You see yourself in light of who God says you are in His written Word," says Wilhite.[2]

Loss of self. After a breakup a few years ago with a man she really loved, Barbara was devastated. She felt like a part of her was missing, like it was taken from her in a bad case of emotional identity theft. He took, but she also "gave it all away"—physically and emotionally, body and soul, before she had the commitment of marriage. She often felt needy around a man and incomplete without one.

Instead of being misaligned, you may feel like your self-esteem has been misplaced altogether. You feel lost because you lost yourself in the relationship. Maybe you were a people pleaser, a "yes" girl, and now you're uncertain as to your identity and purpose. *Who am I apart from you? Who am I now?* Maybe you spent so much time on his life that you neglected your own.

He may have left you, but *you* left you as well, and you abandoned yourself.

Like the walking dead, you can tell when the light has gone out in someone's life. You can see it in the vacant look in their eyes, their house of self is empty, and no one is home. They don't smile often. They may seem disconnected or listless, bitter or cynical. Or just plain sad.

Loss of self means you are out of touch with what you need and want. It is the ultimate abandonment when you don't feel worthy to live in your own life. Your heart is like a deserted house, dark and empty, with boarded up windows and a fence in disrepair.

Stuck in the past. When hurtful memories from the past linger too long in your heart, they can wreak havoc on your self-esteem in the present. An example from classic literature is the eccentric Miss Havisham in *Great Expectations.* Jilted on her wedding day, Miss Havisham was so devastated that she left all the clocks in her house at twenty minutes to nine (because that was the time she received the heartbreaking news from her fiancé), and she never changed them again. This woman held on to her hurt for years by leaving everything as it was on that dreadful day: the decaying remains of the wedding banquet littered the table, and she continued to wear the faded wedding dress. Every day she stared at painful reminders of the past as she clung tightly to "what could have been." Feeling her life was ruined, she let her house and herself live in ruin.

REBUILDING SELF-ESTEEM

How do you stop the "wearing away" of emotional erosion? How do you rebuild self-esteem and restore confidence?

Plant seeds of truth. After a devastating forest fire, erosion is contained by planting grass seed or groundcover and building retaining walls. After a breakup, emotional erosion is shored up by planting seeds of truth and building supportive walls around your heart to retain the truth and prevent future erosion.

The seeds of truth come from reading and hearing God's Word, planting them in your heart, and applying them to your life. In time there is growth, heart hedges holding your life in place—rooted and established. A key verse in Ephesians explains:

I pray that out of his glorious riches he may strengthen you with power through his Spirit in your inner being, so that Christ may dwell in your hearts through faith. And I pray that you, being *rooted and established in love*, may have power, together with all the saints, to grasp how wide and long and high and deep is the love of Christ, and to know this love that surpasses knowledge—that you may be filled to the measure of all the fullness of God. (Ephesians 3:16–19, emphasis mine)

Rooted in God's love and what He says about you, you can stand firm when you feel like your self-worth is being washed away by the strong winds of someone else's unkindness or how your hair turned out that day. When your roots go deep into the source of life, the water of God's Word, you stay fresh and growing. Psalm 1 talks about a man who reads, meditates on, and delights in the Word of God: "He is like a tree planted by streams of water, which yields its fruit in season and whose leaf does not wither. Whatever he does prospers" (v. 3).

Whether you were raised in a family where you were rooted and established in a loving environment or not, God can heal the hurt from your past. "Established in love" means your self-esteem is grounded in God and you begin to grasp God's incredible love for you. A lifetime is not long enough to comprehend the length and depth of God's love; it is longer than the Nile River (4,184 miles long) and deeper than the deepest part of the ocean (35,840 feet below sea level).

Plant seeds of truth and as they grow, you will be better able to take hold of your true identity—what God says about who you are.

Know your true identity. What is your identity? Is it what your driver's license says? Is it what you tell yourself, what others say about you, or what the world thinks? How you see yourself affects how you feel and how you act. It affects your level of confidence.

Let's sort out what self-image, self-esteem, and identity mean. *Self-image* is how you see yourself. It is *your* perception of you. Your self-image includes how you view things like your appearance (height, weight, age), gender, personality, education, skills, abilities, job success, and more. Often our earliest influences of self image come from the input of parents, family, and friends, and also from teachers, coaches, and those in ministry. Other people may say things about you that contribute to how you view yourself but you may not believe them, or they may be wrong.

> THOSE IN THE world have a confused standard for value and worth. They drape themselves to hide their emptiness while we purify ourselves to gain transparency. They hide while we shine.
> —Lisa Bevere

The input that forms your identity comes not only from what you tell yourself and what others have told you that you are, but also from the accuser (Revelation 12:10). Day and night the enemy of your soul strives to mess up your sense of self with lies and deception. That's why it's so crucial to plant seeds of God's truth in your heart and water them with the Word. As you live out truth, your roots will grow deep and provide stability and security to withstand opposition.

Popular culture also tries to shape your self-image—every second of the day— with alluring advertising that demands, in so many words, "This is who you should be: Be thin, be smart, *and* beautiful, have a perfect smile and flawless skin, then you will be loved. You will be significant. You will be somebody."

In *The True Measure of a Woman*, Lisa Bevere says this:

> Those in the world have a confused standard for value and worth. They drape themselves to hide their emptiness while we purify ourselves to gain transparency. They hide while we shine.[3]

So often we want to hide the broken and less-than-perfect parts of our selves. Yet as we come to realize that Christ loves us in the middle of our mess, that startling love helps us to accept both our strengths and weaknesses, both the dark and light, and our self-image becomes less broken and more whole. His power in our weakness (2 Corinthians 12:9).

Self-esteem is the value you place on how you see yourself. It's how content you are with that image. Of course, self-esteem fluctuates, but if it is too high, it can lead to a prideful heart. Perhaps you've seen a woman who thinks she is "all that." Her smugness and conceit is contrasted with the person who has low self-esteem, who thinks she is "none of that." She focuses more on her mistakes instead of what she does right. She is often unsure or fearful, and her insecurity prevents her from speaking up, taking chances, or moving forward.

Whether it's too high or too low, ask yourself if your assessment of your self or situation is accurate. Ask God to give you insight. Romans 12:3 states, "For by the grace given me I say to every one of you: Do not think of yourself more highly than you ought, but rather think of yourself with sober judgment, in accordance with the measure of faith God has given you."

Strive for a balanced view of yourself. A woman with a healthy self-esteem respects herself. She feels secure and worthwhile because of what God says about her. She has confidence in relationships and in life and generally more joy. She knows she has significance; she matters. With her sense of worth and value intact, she sits up straight and walks tall. Her head up, this confident woman is friendly, gentle, and kind. She makes eye contact when she speaks, and she doesn't constantly apologize for everything she says or does.

After a breakup, you may feel like your self-esteem has plummeted because rejection can make you feel unwanted, unloved, or unworthy. It's hard to learn to trust again and you wonder about your judgment. Often women wonder "what is wrong with me?" when in reality a man has not beheld your true worth. And neither have you.

When a relationship ends, some people find it extremely difficult to unfasten themselves from a guy and release the love tie. You know it's over but letting go is excruciating. Perhaps it is the fear of change, or fear of being alone that makes it hard to separate. Maybe it goes deeper, and you think you will never find love again, or you're not even worthy of a "good" relationship.

That's when it's time to stop and think about what you are telling yourself. "Other people, circumstances, events and material things are *not* what make you happy," said William Backus and Marie Chapian in *Telling Yourself the Truth.* "What you *believe* about these things is what makes you happy or unhappy."[4] For example, the authors say that if you believe that no one talking to you at a dinner party would be a horrible situation, then you will act accordingly. You will feel tense, nervous, or uncomfortable.

In fact, something similar happened to me years ago. Alex and I had an unhealthy relationship from the start, and almost two years later I was still tolerating his immature behavior. He had just moved to another state and one evening we went to dinner with his new friends. We sat outdoors under a clear southwestern sky on an adobe patio with white lights. During the course of the evening, he completely ignored me. Not one word. Near the end of the meal I went to the ladies room and looked in the mirror. My hair looked great that night, my makeup was fine, and I had on a nice outfit. *What is wrong with me? Why doesn't he pay any attention to me?*

I was telling myself (without really knowing it) that a man's care for me was based on my appearance, and that what *he* thought or said mattered most. I was putting more weight on what Alex thought than what God said about me—that I was lovable and I was worthy of being treated with appreciation and respect, with true attention and consistent care.

What I came to learn later on was that Alex was a "yo-yo guy." He was constantly up and down and didn't treat me well consistently. I also learned that my self-worth was not based on what he or any man thought of me; I had value whether Mr. Self Absorbed affirmed it or not.

It's important to remember that your value is not based on what one man thinks about you. This anonymous post sent to me recently says it well:

Women are like apples on trees. The best are at the top of the tree. But most men don't want to reach for the good ones because they are afraid of falling and getting hurt. Instead, they sometimes take the apples from the ground; they aren't as good, but they're easy. *The apples at the top think something's wrong with them, when in reality, they're amazing.* They just have to wait for the right man to come along, the one who is brave enough to climb all the way to the top of the tree. (emphasis mine)

As you allow God to shift your self-esteem from how you see yourself to seeing your worth and value through God's eyes, a realignment takes place. God empowers you to see differently, and you begin to act differently. Your perception changes—and so does your life.

Identity asks the question, "Who am I?" Your personal identity, which is closely related to your self-image, is what makes you uniquely you. It is who you are, but it can be transformed into who you aspire to be.

After a relationship breakup a common question in going from a couple to a single is "Who am I now?" You want to know if you are loveable and worthy. How do you find your way forward on your own?

Isabella lost herself in her last relationship. Everyone knew her as "Jake's girlfriend." In fact, she had been part of a couple for so long that she didn't know who she was anymore.

Marisa often changed her personality to be whatever the guy she was dating at the time wanted because she thought it would make him like her more. She would simply rearrange herself to suit a man's tastes like the Mr. Potato Head toy with interchangeable parts. After her last relationship ended, Marisa was at a loss to define her own preferences and personality.

Before she got married, a friend of mine wrestled with her identity as she contemplated the decision to change her last name to her husband's. She loved him dearly and wanted to honor him by taking his name, but where she grew up her maiden name carried a lot of weight in the community—her family name was a part of her heritage and her identity of success.

Are you who you date? Are you what you do for a living? Are you who your last name says you are? What will you do if those things change; then who are you?

I lived most of my adult life in Milwaukee and for twelve years I worked in corporate marketing for a large company. Then my life changed radically. I felt God's leading to move to Colorado and become a freelance writer. It led me to question a lot of things about my identity: "Apart from this job, this place, these friends, who am I?"

Once I was going through some hard times financially and worked for a few months as a pizza delivery girl. I'd ring the doorbell in an upscale neighborhood and the customer would often look past me instead of at me. How could they possible know who I really was underneath my outfit and cap? But I knew. It was as if I wore an invisible badge that read "Ambassador for Christ" and "Aspiring Author" only they couldn't see it.

As I learned more about what God had to say about me, I discovered that my true identity was not in my clothes or my salary. It wasn't in how much money I gave to church or how hard I worked to earn favor with God or with a man I wanted to date. "It is not what we do that determines who we are. It is who we are that determines what we do," says Neil T. Anderson in *The Bondage Breaker*.[5] "I don't do the things I do with the hope that God may one day love me," he continues, "God loves me, and that is why I do what I do."[6]

Breakups can affect your self-esteem and your identity. When you look at yourself, you may have a clear picture or a distorted image—either way it's your point of view. With the yardstick the world uses, you may feel like you will never measure up. However, when God looks at your life, He sees something entirely different—and His point of view is authenticity, reality, and truth.

YOUR IDENTITY IN GOD'S EYES

So often a woman looks to a man to affirm her worth and value. If he thinks she is great, she feels great. If he doesn't, her worth withers. We are sorely deceived when we think that any man has the final answer to our significance. "No man can tell you who you are as a woman. No man is the verdict on your soul," say

John and Stasi Eldredge in *Captivating.* "Only God can tell you who you are. Only God can speak the answer you need to hear."[7]

To be sure, the authors affirm that it's normal in a loving relationship to speak well of each other. It's important to affirm each other with words. However, they conclude, our "*core* validation, our *primary* validation has to come from God."[8]

You may have many roles in your life: sister, friend, daughter, single parent, coworker, Bible study leader, basketball coach, or a number of other roles. If you've been crushed in love one too many times you may feel like you have the role of victim, loser, or reject. But what does God have to say about who you are? In God's eyes, you are:

His friend. "Greater love has no one than this, that he lay down his life for his friends. You are my friends if you do what I command. I no longer call you servants, because a servant does not know his master's business. Instead, I have called you friends, for everything that I learned from my Father I have made known to you" (John 15:13–15).

A child of God—an adopted son or daughter. Your heavenly Father doesn't just tolerate you; He lavishes love upon you. "How great is the love the Father has lavished on us, that we should be called children of God! And that is what we are!" (1 John 3:1).

As a child of God you can retain your *childlike* ways of wonder and humility, but not be *childish*—immature, irresponsible, or self-indulgent. First Corinthians 13:11 admonishes, "When I was a child, I talked like a child, I thought like a child, I reasoned like a child. When I became a man, I put childish ways behind me."

Princess. Because your Father God is the King of kings (Revelation 17:14) you are a princess or prince. You have rights and responsibilities as a member of the royal family to love, give, and serve. You are an heir (Galatians 4:7) "and you have an inheritance that can never perish, spoil or fade" (1 Peter 1:4).

Bride of Christ. The church is the bride of Christ, waiting for the Bridegroom to return (Ephesians 5:25–27). Until He does, we are to make ourselves ready to be with the Bridegroom (Revelation 19:6–8), not with a Vera Wang gown but clothed in purity and dignity and strength.

The Bible has many other things to say about your true identity and how God sees you. You are precious, honored, and highly valued (Isaiah 43:14). You are the apple of His eye (Zechariah 2:8), someone who is held dear. You are chosen (Isaiah 41:9), you are accepted by God (Romans 15:7), you belong to Him (1 Peter 2:9), and you are loved with an everlasting love, one that never ends (Jeremiah 31:3).

The light of Christ brings illumination. Once you've discovered your true identity, who you are in God's eyes, and choose to live in that truth, you will begin to see yourself in a whole new light. You reawaken to who you really are—chosen, accepted, and dearly loved—and find the courage to be yourself. "The closer we get to God, the more clearly we will see ourselves as we really are," says Nancy Leigh DeMoss in *Brokenness*.[9]

When your identity is rooted and grounded in what God says about you, your self-esteem is more solid. You are better able to handle success or failure, deal with change, make decisions, and move forward to give and receive real and lasting love.

Retaining your identity. In relationships, learning to bond and to separate are essential skills. As you get to know another person, you share more about yourself and you develop deeper levels of closeness. You connect.

Dr. Henry Cloud calls bonding one of our most basic and foundational needs. He affirms that we are relational at our very core, and God created us with a hunger for connection and relationships. "Bonding is the ability to establish an emotional attachment to another person," says Cloud. "It's the ability to relate to another on the deepest level."[10] When we feel more connected to others, whether it's a romantic or other kind of relationship, we are happier and healthier.

The other side of the coin is learning how to separate and keep your sense of self intact in the process, whether you are in a relationship or not. "Separateness is an important aspect of human identity," says Cloud. "We are to be connected to others without losing our own identity and individuality . . . to master the art of 'being me without losing you.'"[11]

When you retain your sense of self and the man keeps his identity intact, you will be a better couple. In essence, when each person's sense of "me" is solid, there is a better "we." For instance, think of two circles side by side—one is yellow (representing you) and the other is blue (representing the man). When a couple first meets, the circles touch on the outer limit; their lives have not yet intersected. Then as they get to know each other, the overlapping part that represents them as a couple becomes increasingly green (because yellow and blue make green). If they marry and become one, the two circles mesh to form one circle that is entirely green. The point is, each person must retain his or her sense of self in order for a healthy couple to exist; he must keep his blue-ness and she must retain her yellow-ness, otherwise green won't happen.

Changing your identity. In the Bible, there once was a man named Saul who persecuted Jesus' followers. The story is recorded in Acts 9. He had an amazing life transformation one day as he walked the road to Damascus. A light flashed around him, God spoke to him, and he was never the same. His identity changed dramatically from someone who was out to destroy people who followed Jesus to one of the most influential men and missionaries in history. He also authored a number of books in the New Testament. His identity changed, and eventually his name changed to Paul.

The Lord wants to transform your identity, too. Not to take away who you are, but to reveal who you really are. No longer a slave, you are a friend. No longer an orphan, you are a child of God. Instead of a pauper, a princess; instead of alone and unloved, a bride.

> THE LORD WANTS to transform your identity, too. Not to take away who you are, but to reveal who you really are.

Don't let your pain or your past define you. It is a part of who you are, but it's not the entirety of what makes you the unique individual you are. Who you once were, or who you are now can be transformed as your identity comes from your security in Christ.

RESTORING CONFIDENCE

When your identity is rooted in the soil of God's truth, your confidence grows. So when you run into the guy who dumped you, or the girl he is with now, it won't shatter your self-esteem. Sure, it may shake you up a bit at first, but you bend; you don't break. As you learn to accept your strengths and your weaknesses, you build the confidence that you are worth being loved well.

Confidence is very attractive. In fact, I've heard a number of men say that it's not always how a woman looks that first attracts them. Surprising as that may be, they say that it's her *confidence* and how she makes them feel.

One day down the road you may start dating again, and when you do, you will have the confidence to move forward and make better choices next time (more about that in chapter 11). You will be trusting and walking by faith—confident in God, and His abilities, not your inabilities. Confident, because God is faithful. "The one who calls you is faithful and he will do it" (1 Thessalonians 5:24).

PRAYER

Lord, I need new confidence and self-esteem after this time of rejection. Help me to focus on You, not my circumstances. Plant seeds of truth in my life and help them to grow so I can know my true identity based on what You say and what You see. When the words or actions of others hurt me, please shore up my eroded self-esteem. Give me clarity and true perspective. Help me to find renewed confidence. In Jesus' name, Amen.

LIGHT FOR THE JOURNEY

Here are some suggestions to improve self-esteem and build confidence:

- Challenge negative and "what is wrong with me?" thinking.
- Watch your "self-talk" and ruminating. Oftentimes we are harder on ourselves than others are.
- Appreciate your positive strengths and work on areas that may need improvement.
- Stay away from critical and negative people as much as possible.
- Don't put yourself down, build yourself up with God's Word.

- Accept compliments graciously. Just say, "thank you."
- Face your fears with faith.
- Don't be afraid to say no.
- When your self-esteem starts to crash, ask yourself: What happened? Is it true? What evidence is leading me to that conclusion? Then consider if you need to change something in your life, or let go of what happened.
- Know that what one person thinks about you is just one person's opinion.
- Love and respect yourself.
- Remember: you are worth being loved well!
- Handle with humor; find something to laugh about.

ILLUMINATION

1. What is one of your earliest experiences of rejection?

2. What is one thing about your last breakup (during or after it) that has affected your self-esteem the most?

3. What is your personal identity based upon—what others say about you or what God says about you?

4. List three things you like about yourself. List three things you would like to improve.

Part 4:
Day

10 Arise: Waking Up to the Rest of Your Life

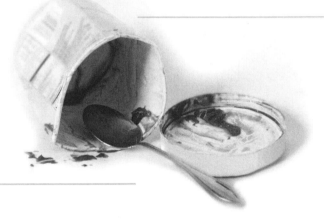

Arise, shine, for your light has come, and the glory of the Lord rises upon you. —Isaiah 60:1

Finally, it is day. It's a time of new beginnings. As the sun rises, you delight in the fact that a broken heart is not incurable; God makes all things new. How amazing it is to know that every day is a chance to start fresh and begin again.

However, in your heart-healing journey some areas of your life may have been neglected as you've been focusing inward on your own personal pain. Valid as that is, living "beyond the breakup" and finding your way forward means paying attention to things you may have put on the back burner or ignored for some time.

God is calling you to step into the day. It's time to wake up and attend to the rest of your life.

Some of the areas that may need attention could include the desire to revive friendships that have fallen away or build some new ones. You want to reengage in life again and make solid connections. With renewed hope you remember again what you really enjoy, and you start doing those hobbies or activities again. As you look to God, He will give you renewed vision and passion for His good purposes, like serving others and using your gifts and talents in work and ministry opportunities.

Don't wait for someone else to make your life better. As you put God first and walk on with Him, He will reveal your next steps. God first, then other things (Matthew 6:33). Your future may include a new boyfriend or a husband some day, or it may not. Only God knows. For now, serve God, love others, and watch what happens next.

CHANGING YOUR LIFE

Recently I was driving downtown and at a stoplight I spotted the city's old train station across the street. It had once been a bustling transportation hub, but over time the facility was abandoned and fell into disrepair. Years later someone had the bright idea to renovate the old building, and now the once-defunct train station has been transformed into offices and stylish lofts.

Transformation. Change. It was time for some fixing up in my own life.

After a breakup a few years ago, I had been so consumed with my own misery and getting over a guy, that I almost forgot who I was and what I wanted—and what God wanted for me. Slowly I began to wake up and remember that I wanted to write, to travel, and to get my finances in order so I could be a generous giver.

I could tell a fresh wind of change was blowing in my life because as I emerged from the breakup blues, I suddenly got the urge to spring clean everything—and it wasn't even springtime. I got rid of clothes that no longer fit or were no longer in style. I wanted to redecorate and did a few small things to my place. I was changing and I wanted my environment around me to change, too.

IS IT TIME for new purposes, new visions, and new dreams in your life? Are there things you want to change?

Is it time for new purposes, new visions, and new dreams in your life? Are there things you want to change? Like a winter coat in July, it may be time to shed some old ways of thinking, like negative self-talk or put-downs. Maybe you want to lose weight or take a class—not because some guy is telling you to change, but because you want to do it for yourself.

Take this time to focus on what you want to be different in your life: get in touch with friends, learn more about how men "work," or update your wardrobe. Out with the old, in with the new. No matter what you discard, don't ever throw away the outfit that looks good on everyone and never goes out of style:

> Therefore, as God's chosen people, holy and dearly loved, *clothe yourselves* with compassion, kindness, humility, gentleness and patience. Bear with each other and forgive whatever grievances you may have against one another. Forgive as the Lord forgave you. And over all these virtues put on love, which binds them all together in perfect unity. (Colossians 3:12–14, emphasis mine)

Living beyond your breakup begins as you wake up to the rest of your life and arise to gratitude, to community, to joy, to serving others, to vision and purpose, and to adventure—learning to trust again and take risks.

ARISE TO GRATITUDE

You've been through a lot to get from breakup to better days in your heart-healing journey. You've survived disappointment, discouragement, and maybe even depression. When you arise to gratitude, your thankful heart soars higher than your circumstances. A grateful heart cries, "Thank You for all You have done for me, Lord."

As you begin to chart a new course in life, remember the darkness from which you came and thank God for the light—the goodness, peace, and joy—you finally have in your heart. Even if all the hurt has not yet been loved away, thank Him for how far you've come. Here are some good Bible verses to remember about thankfulness:

Give thanks always. "Always giving thanks to God the Father for everything, in the name of our Lord Jesus Christ." (Ephesians 5:20)

Give thanks because God is good. "Give thanks to the Lord, for he is good; his love endures forever." (Psalm 118:1)

Give thanks for God's unfailing love. "Then they cried to the Lord in their trouble, and he saved them from their distress. He brought them out of darkness and the deepest gloom and broke away their chains. Let them give thanks to the Lord for his unfailing love and his wonderful deeds for men." (Psalm 107:13–15)

Give thanks because we have victory. "But thanks be to God! He gives us the victory through our Lord Jesus Christ." (1 Corinthians 15:57)

ARISE TO COMMUNITY

After a breakup, singles often feel lonely or disconnected from other people. Isolation can lead to a lack of motivation and a lot less joy. Instead of trying to be tough and self-sufficient, know that it's okay to rely on others, especially people who are affirming, accepting, and trustworthy.

We were created for connection. Yet oftentimes we don't have the energy for it if we are too focused on our own problems, or we haven't taken the time to develop quality friendships. Sadly, TV shows can become a quick fix for company since these people show up in your living room at least once a week. But TV is only a one-way connection.

Our pastor once said that if God can separate you from authentic community, then you are easy prey for the Enemy because you are isolated and alone. Whether it's with your family, friends, church, book club, Bible study, sports team, community theater group, scrapbooking club, or other types of community, we all need real, live, human contact.

Of course, solitude can be healing and we all need some time to ourselves, but we need to find a balance between being alone and being with other people—not just with online friends, but face-to-face personal interaction.

Indeed, restoration often comes within relationships. Being in healthy and supportive relationships other than dating connections can be very healing. As people treat you with kindness and treat you well, they reinforce the truths you've learned that you are worthy and have infinite value. Proverbs 27:17 says, "As iron sharpens iron, so one man sharpens another."

Plus, you may be able to help someone else in their time of need after their breakup because you can relate and empathize. You can offer them hope and comfort and help bring healing to others from your own wounding and heart-healing path.

When Erica went through a painful divorce, she was fortunate to have church members who provided practical help as well as a lot of support and encouragement.

People were constantly giving her invitations to their home for meals and fellowship. It helped her to feel less sad and alone and very loved by her church community as they modeled the body of Christ to her. Some of the men in the church volunteered to work on her home (which was in disrepair) and mow her lawn. One of the deacons was a CPA and he helped her with financial planning after the divorce. In addition, she received lots of prayer and letters of encouragement. Erica was extremely grateful as her church loved her in a way she'd never felt loved before.

In fact, what the church did for Erica was a testimony to the community. As she went through the grieving process and was supported in such tangible and kind ways, those outside the church looked on in wonder and amazement.

ARISE TO JOY

After being sad for so long, you've probably wondered when you would feel joy again. Psalm 126:5 says, "Those who sow in tears will reap with songs of joy." It's a new season in your heartland. It's time to remember joy.

As you get further down the heart-healing road from the breakup pain to brighter days, joy returns. You remember how good it feels to laugh. And you find delight in playing with your sister's kids or your friend's new puppy. You awaken from the dark times that have been consuming you, and you remember what you really enjoy, what makes you happy, and you start doing those things again—like listening to jazz music or riding your bike.

When something is a delight and makes me feel really good, I call it a "raspberry moment." It happens to me when I eat fresh raspberries; they make me happy because I have good memories associated with eating them.

It's funny how one bite of the little red fruit and suddenly I am eight years old again. I can see my little girl self walking across the gravel road in front of my grandparents' summer cabin in the Wisconsin north woods toward a long patch of wild raspberries. We'd pick them and eat them on cereal or right from the vine when we just couldn't wait. I can get lost in thinking about those long summer days of freedom and adventure—just me and my two sisters with my maternal grandparents for two weeks every summer. Bliss!

Is there something in your life that's a "raspberry moment" for you? What makes you feel really good when you think about it and fills you with joy?

ARISE TO SERVING OTHERS

I think it was Mark Twain who said, "The best way to cheer yourself up is to try to cheer somebody else up."

After a relationship ended in Barbara's life, she discovered that serving others took the focus off herself and her own problems while also building God's kingdom. She said, "It felt right, and it gave me purpose." Despite her circumstances, Barbara found that when she was blessing others with acts of service and kindness, God blessed her with joy. Instead of waiting for another man to come around, she could "wait on" or serve others. "Like a waitress who serves other people, I can *wait* on God while waiting on God," she concluded.

The Bible says that whatever we do for others, we essentially do for Jesus Christ (Matthew 25:40). I have to remember that my life is not just about me. It's more than that. God created us for Himself and part of that is serving other people. "For we are God's workmanship, created in Christ Jesus to do good works, which God prepared in advance for us to do" (Ephesians 2:10).

The reason we serve, though, is not because good works will save our souls. No, God gave us grace for that. It's not to earn points for favor with God. We serve others because God asks us to and because He has done so much for us. It is out of a heart of delight, not just duty, that we choose to serve others.

So we go on mission trips, not just to tell, but to demonstrate love to a ten-year-old boy in the Czech Republic who has never heard of God's love. We show up on Saturday mornings at the rescue mission to serve food to those who don't have enough to eat. Or even, like my friend Anne, offer to drive our nonchurched friends to church so they can hear the truth and be forever changed.

If you spend yourselves in behalf of the hungry and satisfy the needs of the oppressed, then your light will rise in the darkness, and your night will become like the noonday. (Isaiah 58:10)

Think of the Christian life as a two-sided sponge—the spongy side absorbs the water and the rough, green side scrubs. Likewise, we *absorb* God's truth (through reading the Bible, hearing a speaker, or reading a book, for example) and then we go out and *serve*. First the Word, then the work.

You may be surprised at the divine appointments God puts in your path as you open your eyes to the needs around you. It doesn't even have to be an organized service project. Serving can include something as simple as being kind to the woman behind the counter at the dry cleaners. When you take the time to say "hello" and smile, even when you think you are in too much of a hurry, it can make a difference in one person's day.

Dwight L. Moody once said, "I am only one, but I am one. I cannot do everything, but I can do something. And that which I can do, by the grace of God, I will do."

What are you willing to do to serve God by serving others today?

ARISE TO VISION AND PURPOSE

God has uniquely crafted you to fulfill His good purposes. In addition to serving others, we were made to worship God, to enjoy Him, and to find and fulfill our callings in work, ministry, and life.

But sometimes we can be weighed down with the heavy rocks of grief, anger, or unresolved conflict. We can be carrying a grudge, feelings of inferiority, or a self-centered versus an other-centered orientation. Whatever the rocks are that you carry, they may be holding you back from moving forward.

Maybe you think you're not good at anything. You don't have any special talents—at least ones that have not yet been recognized. When you think you can't, when you think that you have nothing to offer, remember what someone told me recently, "God doesn't call the *equipped*, He equips the *called*." When God calls you to do something, you can either hang up and ignore it, or you can listen, step out in faith, and allow Him to furnish the resources you'll need to get the job done.

You were created by God and for Him (Colossians 1:16). He crafted you with your unique intellect, creativity, and personality to use your talents and develop your gifts.

> Just as each of us has one body with many members, and these members do not all have the same function, so in Christ we who are many form one body, and each member belongs to all the others. We have different gifts, according to the grace given us. If a man's gift is prophesying, let him use it in proportion to his faith. If it is serving, let him serve; if it is teaching, let him teach; if it is encouraging, let him encourage; if it is contributing to the needs of others, let him give generously; if it is leadership, let him govern diligently; if it is showing mercy, let him do it cheerfully. (Romans 12:4–8)

I've heard that baseball players mentally prepare themselves for a game by picturing in their mind the steps they will take during the game to win it. They see themselves winning it. What do you envision for the next stage of your life? For years down the road? Why not picture yourself joyful. Envision laughing with friends, enjoying family, and doing what you love best. You may even want to write down what you envision.

What is your passion? What do you dream of doing in life, work, or ministry? Take some time to find out what your spiritual gifts are so you can use them. Consider getting a life coach to help you sort out your choices.

God is calling you to something in this new season of your life—what will your answer be?

ARISE TO ADVENTURE

In college I had a poster in my room that read, "A ship in a harbor is safe, but that is not what ships are meant for." Ships are designed to go somewhere; they are for adventures, not dry dock. Certainly, there is a time when a ship may need to be pulled out of the water for needed repairs. But it doesn't stay there. In stormy weather or smooth seas, sunshine or rain, it sails on.

> IF GOD IS the Captain of your life, then trust is built and fear subsides because you know that He is entirely reliable, dependable, and true.

Yet oftentimes people who've had their hearts broken want to stay in the safety of the harbor instead of risking setting sail in the high seas of love again. Theodore Roosevelt once said this about taking risks: "Far better it is to *dare mighty things*, to win *glorious triumphs*, even though checkered by failure, than to rank with those poor spirits who neither *enjoy* much nor suffer much because they live in the gray twilight that knows neither *victory* nor defeat" (emphasis mine).

Beginning again can be challenging. You've been hurt and you don't want to risk having your heart broken again. You've gotten used to the still waters of the harbor; it's quiet, comfortable, and safe. But it's existing, not living. And it takes a leap of faith to put the boat out to sea again.

"The leap of faith always means loving without expecting to be loved in return, giving without wanting to receive, inviting without hoping to be invited, holding without asking to be held," says Henri Nouwen in *The Return of the Prodigal Son*. "And every time I make a little leap, I catch a glimpse of the One who runs out to me and invites me into his joy, the joy in which I can find not only myself, but also my brothers and sisters."[1]

Instead of a blind leap, you take an informed leap of faith because you know who is steering the ship of your life. If God is the Captain of your life, then trust is built and fear subsides because you know that He is entirely reliable, dependable, and true. And He is yours. "But I trust in you, O Lord; I say, 'You are my God'" (Psalm 31:14).

As you learn to take purposeful and prayerful risks and trust again, you will set sail on some amazing new adventures in life. Venture out. Journey on. With your competent and seasoned Captain, who knows what adventures await?

PRAYER

Lord, thank You for a new day. In this new season of my life, help me learn to live "beyond the breakup" and move forward. You have done so much for me and I am truly thankful. Will You help me to wake up to the rest of my life and build community and friendships? Teach me how to find more joy, serve others, awaken to vision and purpose for my life, and trust again. In Jesus' name, Amen.

LIGHT FOR THE JOURNEY

Create a "dream sheet," a list of things you'd like to do now that you may have neglected. To help clarify your vision and purpose for what is next, you may want to add to that sheet by either making a list or writing in story form how you see yourself a year from now, or five years from now. Then pray and ask for direction and favor. Psalm 37:5–6 reads, "Commit your way to the Lord; trust in him and he will do this: He will make your righteousness shine like the dawn, the justice of your cause like the noonday sun."

ILLUMINATION

1. List some things you want to change in your life (e.g., lose weight, spend more time with God, stop being so negative, take a class, travel, start a business, etc.).

2. Think of a time when you were happy and list a "raspberry moment."

3. What can you do to reach out and serve someone in need today?

4. How comfortable are you about taking risks and moving forward in life?

11 Shine: Making Healthier Choices Next Time

Let the morning bring me word of your
unfailing love, for I have put my trust in you.
Show me the way I should go,
for to you I lift up my soul.
—Psalm 143:8

It's morning in your heart-healing journey. The promise of a new day awaits you, a chance for new beginnings. A blank slate. An opportunity, if you take it, to learn about making better choices next time in love and relationships.

The presence of light changes your perception. Without the darkness to obscure your vision, you can see clearly. You don't fall or bump into things because of the dimness. In the same way, the light of God's truth enables you to "see" spiritually. In the Psalms we learn that, "Your word is a lamp to my feet and a light for my path" (Psalm 119:105). No more hiding in the shadows of the past—whether they were your own poor choices or things others have said or done to you.

You can choose to follow the true light (John 1:9), Jesus Christ, or the false lights of worldly wisdom that seek to entice and mislead. But when it comes to taking advice, make sure you know the difference between what's counterfeit and what's true. For example, a well-meaning friend may tell you to "just get out there" and start dating; it doesn't matter whether he is a believer or not. She may sincerely want the best for you, but she may also be sincerely wrong. False lights eventually burn out while God's lasting truth shines on.

With the light of Christ, holes in your heart are exposed. It's normal to feel an empty space in your life when a person you loved (or liked) is no longer there, but when we try to fill it with lies, half-truths, or unhealthy things, the emptiness remains.

Mia, a thirtysomething sales executive in Chicago, thought that having a boyfriend would make her life complete. When someone loved her, she felt good about herself. When he didn't, her self-worth plummeted. Only with a man in her life did she feel satisfied. For a while a new relationship would seem to assuage her heart hunger, but then she'd grow relationally hungry for more and the hole returned.

Often we try to fill our heart with what another person thinks, says, or does when it was meant to be filled by God. He won't let anyone be our total fulfillment; otherwise we wouldn't need Him.

The Lord "fills the hungry with good things" (Psalm 107:9), the physically hungry and the heart hungry. It's not wrong to want a relationship with a man. God is all about relationships and He desires us to be in connection and find community. As we put God first in our heart affections, He fills up the emptiness and we are able to receive the love of others, retain it, and give it away.

> AS WE PUT God first in our heart affections, He fills up the emptiness and we are able to receive the love of others, retain it, and give it away.

Perhaps you think because God hasn't given you someone new to love, that He doesn't care or that He's forgotten about your desires. God is not forgetful, tired, or uncaring. He is constantly at work in the lives of His children, and everything God does is for a reason—even His divine delays.

Now that you are getting over Mr. Wonderful (or Mr.

Wonder-Where-He-Went) you may want to think about how you will do things differently in your next relationship. You can be ready for love again and make wiser and healthier choices by becoming a woman of: wisdom, high standards, realistic expectations, integrity, love, and faith.

BECOME A WOMAN OF WISDOM

Making better choices in relationships begins as you think about the kind of person you want to date and *how* you'll date—the world's way or God's way.

In Western culture, dating is often recreational and includes levels of emotional and physical intimacy (like having sex before marriage) that are contrary to Christian beliefs.

While the word "dating" does not appear in the Bible, it does say that a Christ-follower is to marry a believer. Second Corinthians 6:14 reads, "Do not be yoked together with unbelievers. For what do righteousness and wickedness have in common? Or what fellowship can light have with darkness?"

God's Word does not have an Intro to Dating 101 section. However, we know that He desires people to treat each other with honesty, respect, and honor. Honoring another person following biblical principles means being more other-centered than self-centered, and experiencing physical intimacy after commitment (the commitment of marriage).

It seems wise to get to know someone first to see if you are compatible before you connect in a dating relationship. Spend time with your friends, his friends, or your singles group instead of instant one-on-one time. That way you can prevent heartbreak for both parties if either of you discovers the other person is not for you after all.

We can look at the commands of living a holy life and apply them to all our relationships, including dating and marriage. The book of Ephesians lists a few: "Be completely humble . . . be patient, "bearing with one another" (4:2); "speak truthfully" (4:25); "in your anger do not sin" (4:26); "build up others with your words" (4:29); "get rid of all bitterness" (4:31); "be kind and compassionate . . . , forgiving each other" (4:32); "and live a life of love" (5:2).

Just as natural light dispels the darkness, the light of God's Word reveals truth. Step by step, moment by moment, and choice by choice, your heart is illuminated with understanding and "aha!" moments; you finally get it and begin to change how you see yourself, God, and His role in your love life.

Wisdom is essential in making changes. Without it we do really dumb things that hurt others or ourselves. Wisdom protects, leads, guides, and gives knowledge and understanding. Wisdom gives us victory!

As you follow the path of wisdom, something wonderful happens. You grow upon the inside. When hardships come, like a breakup, it can cause us to wise up and become more emotionally and spiritually mature. What does that kind of person look like?

A mature person loves, accepts, and respects herself. She learns to put rejection and loss in perspective, and trust the bigger picture of God's guiding hand. She deals with issues as they come up and doesn't let them accumulate. Garbage needs to be taken out regularly, and emotional garbage needs to be processed and dumped frequently, too. She doesn't hold on to the past but clings tightly to the Savior who is her future and her hope.

A mature person lives in the *reality* of the present, not the *fantasy* of the past or the future. She doesn't obsess for far too long over a guy who's dumped her or imagine herself in a white dress and veil with someone who is clearly not pursing her. A mature person trusts that God really does know best. And she lives what she believes. James 1:22 says, "Do not merely listen to the word, and so deceive yourselves. Do what it says." Know it, do it, change your life.

When you live in the light of God's truth, you begin to feel stronger and more confident, and you become more equipped to make healthier relationship choices.

TO HAVE THE lasting love
and intimacy you desire, it's
essential to identify unhealthy
patterns in your own life, change
what you can about yourself, and
then come into greater clarity
about the qualities you want
in another person.

What keeps women from making better choices in the men they choose and how they act when they're with them? Selfishness. Rebellion. Ignorance. Apathy. Many things. But it's also important to know that as much as you want to get it right, the Evil One wants you to get it wrong. The Christian life is a constant struggle between good and evil, truth and lies. Your enemy wants you to fail. In fact, he is like a thief who only wants to "steal and kill and destroy" (John 10:10). He wants to steal your joy, kill your dreams, and destroy your relationships.

But take heart; Jesus came so that you "may have life, and have it to the full" (also John 10:10). The Enemy lies to you when you hear that you're not enough. He lies when you feel like you'll never find someone special, that you'll be alone forever, that no one really cares, or that you will never change. Not true. Don't buy into the Evil One's lies. He's been doing it since the garden of Eden. He deceived Eve, and he will try to deceive you. When you know the truth and stand, you can combat the lies and find victory in your love life and your entire life.

BECOME A WOMAN OF HIGH STANDARDS

Often books on relationships emphasize *finding* the right person, but it's also important to *be* the right person. To have the lasting love and intimacy you desire, it's essential to identify unhealthy patterns in your own life, change what you can about yourself, and then come into greater clarity about the qualities you want in another person.

Identify unhealthy patterns. Healthy relationships grow when we know our true identity, who we are in Christ, and respect our individuality and uniqueness. They also flourish when we know and connect with who God is and how that makes a difference in our life. (Chapters 5 and 7 cover these topics in more detail.) We are all made with different habits, personality traits, and ways of relating. However, sometimes we do things in a relationship that hurt ourselves or damage the connection and we don't know why.

Sometimes we know our weak spots and sometimes we are blind-sighted. Danielle works at a major university and she's been a Christian believer for years. Like many women she talks with her friends about men and reads books and articles about them. She thought she had relationships figured out—and then Glenn showed up. He was not on the same page spiritually or emotionally, and she knew he wasn't right for her. Yet little by little he wore her down with his charisma and charming words.

Danielle spent time with him knowing it couldn't go anywhere, and every day her heart got more and more invested in the wrong man. She also knew she was spiritually starving because she hadn't read her Bible (her spiritual food) for months. Hungry for attention, she forgot the wise words in Proverbs 4:23, "Above all else, guard your heart, for it is the wellspring of life." Her affections of the heart were strong and were leading her down a path that only meant trouble. Although she was strong in her faith, she realized that without the firm planting of God's Word as her truth, she was just as vulnerable as the next person.

She knew something had to change, and during the next few months Danielle began to remember where her true value came from; it was God's opinion of her, not a man's that really counted. As she filled her heart with God's promises about her worth and value, and how much God loves her, Danielle became stronger and was able to make better decisions about who she would spend time with in the future.

Think about your past dating experiences. What went wrong? Why did it end? It's helpful to identify any patterns that may be sabotaging the love you desire. You can start by making a list of things you've learned from past relationships—things you've done that you don't want to do again. Here are some examples:

- Stayed too long in a dead-end relationship
- Didn't stand up for yourself when he hurt you with words or actions
- Gave in when he wanted to go farther physically than you wanted to
- Stubbornly wanted your own way all the time
- Didn't know what to do when he treated you poorly
- Lived in a fantasy world of thinking one day "it will be more" when he only wanted friendship
- Pursued him when you should've waited for him to pursue you

♦ Rushed from one relationship to the next when you weren't ready to love again

Change your thoughts and actions. Now that you know what you don't want, it's time to make some changes. What do you want to do differently next time? You don't have to stay stuck in patterns of the past. Ask yourself why you've made unwise relationship choices. If you don't know, then pray and ask God to reveal to you any habits or patterns that have been holding you back. (For more information, see the examples at the end of this chapter in "Light for the Journey.")

Change doesn't have to be scary. You can start by picking one area at a time and doing something, because small steps lead to big changes. By altering what you do, it will change how you think and feel. In his book *Pleasers*, Dr. Kevin Leman affirms that, "when you start changing your behavior, your attitudes, emotions, and feelings will change as well." He suggests, "Ask yourself, *How would the 'old me' react in this situation? How is the 'new me' going to react?*"[1]

Be clear on what you really need in a relationship. My friend Heidi once said, "The difference between the wrong man and the right man is like the difference between the darkest night and the brightest day." In order to make choices that lead to the love and intimacy you desire, it's important to know the characteristics you want—and don't want—in a man. What are your criteria? Think about the kind of men you've picked in the past. What do you want now? What needs to change? Make a list of things you need in a relationship. For instance, "I need

♦ to have a better idea of what I need in another person
♦ to learn to assess more quickly if a man is right for me or not

+ to be clear with myself and the other person what behaviors I will and will not accept
+ someone who is consistent in his words and actions
+ to make time for a quality relationship; to feel more connected
+ a man who will pursue me, be available, and treat me with respect."

THE FIVE Cs FOR FINDING MR. RIGHT

There are many essential traits to look for in a date, and eventually a life partner. I have five listed here, the five Cs: Christian, Communication, Character, Chemistry, and Calling.[2]

Christian means that he has a committed walk with God, he's accepted Jesus as his personal Savior and Lord, and he's on a path of growth and discovery. What else does that mean for you? Do you want someone who will attend church with you every Sunday? Do you want to pray together as a couple? Think about how you want to live out your spiritual life with another person.

Communication is key to any good relationship. It's talking and listening, building rapport and intimacy, sharing, and more. What kind of communication is important to you in a relationship? Are you comfortable going deep in conversation, or do you prefer to stay in the shallow end? What is "good communication" to you?

I remember a dreadful date with a man who did not talk to me almost the entire time we were together. One Sunday afternoon we drove to Green Bay for a Packers football game and he was completely silent throughout the entire game—including halftime! Even the long, soundless drive home was awful. I told myself that day that I needed a man who would not only talk with me but be a good communicator.

Character refers to his temperament, personality, and moral fiber. Does he have integrity? Does he keep his promises, say what he means and mean what he says? How do your personalities mesh? Do you have temperaments that are complementary?

Chemistry is another word for attraction. Is he handsome in your eyes? Does he have qualities that appeal to you? Is there that intangible "certain something" that makes you click as a couple? Of course, chemistry and attraction are important in a relationship, but don't let your feelings dictate your choices based only upon someone's looks. True beauty is more than a perfect smile or fit body. It's both inner and outer qualities, and how that person makes you feel. Additionally, chemistry is just one of the essential five Cs for a healthy and fulfilling match, one piece of the entire love puzzle.

Calling is the term I'll use here for God's vision for your relationship. Is it right for the long term? Has God called you to marriage with this man to be his life partner? You can have all four of the five Cs, but if the "C" of Calling is not there, it will never work.

Finally, before you date someone—whether you meet on the Internet or at the office—make sure he is not married. Seriously. Don't rely on him wearing a ring. Josh had the kind of captivating blue eyes you could dive into and swim laps in for hours. He was a new client at our firm and always stopped by my desk to say hello and chat briefly. Of course, he always had something interesting to say and often I could only eke out pleasantries while I tried to remember my name.

His left-hand ring finger was bare, a good sign. No glint of a gold wedding band to be seen. Since there wasn't a man in my life at the time, I had fun daydreaming about him. It was just for amusement, I told myself. Until the day I learned he was married. Married! Yep. To the same woman for twenty years. Oh, and they have a bunch of kids. *How in the world was that possible?* I mean, he never wore a ring and he was so nice. I was shocked, and surprisingly, a bit hurt. I know I shouldn't have been, but Daydream

Man was gone. Who would I think about now?

It was time to clear my heart and head of even the smallest inklings of desire for this person and get back to what I really wanted—a God-centered lasting love.

BECOME A WOMAN OF REALISTIC EXPECTATIONS

While it's good to have standards and consider the spiritual, intellectual, social, emotional, and physical aspects of your ideal person, it's also wise not to expect perfection. The "right one" will be the one best suited for you if you include God in your love life. Make a list of the qualities you're looking for in a man, and pray about this important choice.

Love will be more successful when you don't expect a man— or anyone—to be faultless. Of course, we know that men and women are different in many ways, so the more we learn about the opposite sex, the greater chance we'll have for better communication, with less frustration and more mutual enjoyment of each other.

In *Finding Mr. Right*, Stephen Arterburn reveals that the *heart* of a man is the most important part of his anatomy. "Often women focus on the wrong traits and mistake character flaws for strengths. They desire the confident, self-assured man, and mistakenly end up with an uncaring and demanding jerk. Wanting strength, they may shun a man who has a sensitive side, who actually is interested in who they are and how to please them." He also says that the wise woman looks for "the inner man who is secure enough to love, free enough to laugh, and humble enough to learn."[3]

It's also important not to have unrealistic expectations about marriage. Some people idealize the fantasy of what they think marriage is supposed to be, and sometimes a reality check is needed.

I have a coworker friend who's been married for over a decade. He and his wife have a large family and, from seeing them at a few work functions, I surmised that they had a happy, strong marriage that was conflict free and breezy. I once said to him, "You guys make it look so easy." His easy grin turned serious when he replied, "It's taken us years to get to this place." *Huh*. I needed to hear that. I needed to know that marriage, like any relationship, has its ups and downs. It takes dedication to live out that kind of commitment.

As challenging as it can be at times, marriage can also be amazing. The bride and the bridegroom are a picture of how Christ loves the church. It's a commitment before God and man to love, honor, and cherish this person all the days of your life— for better or worse. Even when he scatters his clothes on the floor or you are sick. Even when your kids are screaming and you haven't talked to another adult all day. But when you've found someone who accepts you even when you have PMS, and he passionately loves you and loves God with all his heart, you know you've found a really good thing.

As you think and pray about what you want in a life partner, keep a realistic view of marriage, both the bright side and challenging side.

FRIENDSHIP OR DATING—DISCERNING THE DIFFERENCE

Another place to open your eyes and have realistic expectations is in knowing where you stand with a guy. You may be in "The Unknown Zone," the peculiar place between friendship and dating where you don't really know what your relationship is or where you stand. It may turn into something real and lasting, or it may not. How can you know when he doesn't communicate or his signals are mixed?

Michelle McKinney Hammond gets to the heart of the matter in *The Unspoken Rules of Love*. "If he does not ask you to have an exclusive relationship with him, assume that you are not in one."[4] He needs to be initiating and pursuing you. If not, she continues, "Consider and enjoy your other options. Do not behave as if you are in a committed relationship when you are not. Doing so will only entangle your heart and set you up for disappointment and heartbreak. If he doesn't tell you he wants to be in a committed relationship, consider yourself officially 'just a friend.'"[5]

A pastor I know once said, "The proof of desire is in the pursuit." If a man wants to get to know you, you will know his intentions. You won't have to guess. Don't give him excuses like maybe he's busy, maybe he's shy, maybe he's had a family crisis, or maybe (fill in the blank). Bottom line: *For whatever reason* (you don't even have to know what it is), if he is not pursuing you, then you need to let it go. March forward with your life and trust God for the right man for you.

BECOME A WOMAN OF INTEGRITY

Signs and signals are important for our safety on the road and in relationships. Have you ever been in traffic and the car in front of you flashes a bright red *left* turn signal, and then suddenly turns *right*. Um—*what're ya doing?* When a man treats you like that, sends mixed signals, it can be confusing. It's time to ask questions and get clarification. What kinds of signs is he giving you? Does he act like a boyfriend and then treat you like a friend? Does he just want to be physical (sexual) with you, and then acts like he doesn't even know you? If he doesn't pursue you, don't settle for being a "friend with benefits." You deserve better.

Think about this: Lust visits, love stays. Lust takes, love gives. Lust is selfish, love puts the other person first. You can tell over the course of time a man's intentions. "Only time can reveal the difference between infatuation and lasting love," says Bill Hybels in *Fit to Be Tied*.[6]

To be a woman of integrity, go to the source of integrity, the Bible. This helpful and holy book addresses what to do, and not do, with your body before you are married. We are to honor God with our bodies, not degrade them. For instance, 1 Corinthians 6:18–20 says, "Flee from sexual immorality. All other sins a man commits are outside his body, but he who sins sexually sins against his own body. Do you not know that your body is a temple of the Holy Spirit, who is in you, whom you have received from God? You are not your own; you were bought at a price. Therefore honor God with your body." Sex is for two people who've made a commitment, a marriage covenant. In fact, one of the best gifts you can give your husband on your wedding night is yourself. Hebrews 13:4 affirms that, "marriage should be honored by all, and the marriage bed kept pure, for God will judge the adulterer and all the sexually immoral." God's words, not mine.

Sadly, sex before marriage is so prevalent in our contemporary culture that sometimes people forget God intended this intimate expression of love for a lifelong committed relationship called marriage. Not outside of it. In the context of marriage, it's a special and incredible thing that, like a fire in a fireplace, brings warmth, comfort, and joy. In the wrong context, a cozy fire that burns outside of the fireplace's boundaries becomes out of control and sets the house ablaze, damaging your property and destroying your life.

If you've already gone too far sexually, you can find healing and forgiveness. You can become what one woman I know calls, "a born-again virgin." Talk to God about it in prayer. Confess what you've done wrong and ask for His forgiveness. And our gracious God will forgive you and make you clean and pure again. "Love covers over a multitude of sins" (1 Peter 4:8).

EMOTIONAL AND PHYSICAL BOUNDARIES

A few years ago, Scott Croft wrote a column for the Boundless.org website, a Focus on the Family webzine for singles. In it, he talked about how God's Word (in 1 Thessalonians 4:1–8) "admonishes us not to wrong or 'defraud' our brother or sister by implying a marital level of commitment (through sexual involvement) when it does not exist."[7] The passage tells us, among other things, to avoid sexual immorality, control our body in a way that is holy and honorable, not in passionate lust.

Many times women have come to me and said they felt terrible (used, shamed, and hurt) when they gave in to the sexual demands of men who were not their husbands. Whether it was a boyfriend trying to push his limits or just a guy they hooked up with, they were "defrauded" and not treated as they deserved to be—with love, respect, and honor. When someone uses you for his or her own selfish pleasure, no matter what the level of physical intimacy, it is both physically and emotionally inappropriate.

People can wound you with words or with their actions. That's why boundaries are vital in dating and relationships— both the *physical* limits of how far you will or will not go sexually (to guard your body) and *emotional* limits of what you will or will not accept from others verbally and relationally (to guard your heart).

In their classic *Boundaries,* Dr. Henry Cloud and Dr. John Townsend describe the protective device like a fence: "Boundaries help us keep the good in and the bad out. They guard our treasures (Matthew 7:6) so that people will not steal them."[8] Your heart is a treasure, and so is your body.

Guarding your heart means you don't "play house" by acting like you're married when you are not. Doing so can be very hurtful when you break up because the emotional ties you've created now need to be severed. Protect your heart from emotional injuries you were never designed to incur.

What will your boundaries be in your next relationship? How will you enforce them? One wise way is to not spend too much time alone and spend more time in groups or with others.

Another way is to know your boundaries and be strong in your convictions ahead of time.

BECOME A WOMAN OF LOVE

A woman of love makes smarter choices in relationships because she loves God, others, and herself.

Loving yourself means you can *be yourself*, not an exact replica of the man you're dating. You have enough self-respect to not grovel when he says he no longer wants to go out with you. You say "no" when you really don't want to spend time with a guy, instead of leading him on by trying to be nice. You speak the truth in love (Ephesians 4:15).

> LOVING YOURSELF means you can *be yourself*, not an exact replica of the man you're dating.

Loving others starts with Jesus' words, "Love your neighbor as yourself" (Mark 12:31). Like women, men need affirmation, appreciation, and encouragement. They also receive love as you respect them and trust them. Whether you end up dating or marrying a new man, or just seeing him a few times, treat him well—the way you'd want to be treated—with kindness, grace, and forgiveness.

Love God enough to listen to what He says, to follow Him, and to ask for wisdom. Let Him be the first one you run to when you need to make decisions. Love Him enough to trust Him, because He really does know what He's doing even when we do not.

BECOME A WOMAN OF FAITH

Maggie was five months pregnant when the man she adored left her. Single and alone, she cried every day for years until she finally realized that God did not want her to live that way. "For whatever reason," she says, "God rescues us from our desires for reasons we cannot see until much later. You cannot ponder as to why; it is a waste of time and energy. We are to move forward and have faith!" Maggie has learned to move from the shallow end to the deep end of faith. She doesn't timidly dip her toes, she's all in!

Faith is total reliance on the One who is completely reliable. "Know therefore that the Lord your God is God; he is the faithful God, keeping his covenant of love to a thousand generations of those who love him and keep his commands" (Deuteronomy 7:9).

"One way or the other," says Susie Larson in *The Uncommon Woman*, "you are called to faith—the stretching, reaching, I don't-know-if-I-can-do-this kind of faith. And when you shift all of your hopes and dreams into the arms of the Most High God, you will find Him faithful."[9]

Consider praying, even now, for the man God has for you. Pray for his relationship with God, that he will be a man of integrity, a man of his word, communicate well, be loving and affectionate, or whatever you need. Ask God to lead each of you to each other—and when you do eventually meet, that He will protect and guide your relationship.

Remember, God has good things for you. His Word says, "'For I know the plans I have for you,' declares the Lord, 'plans to prosper you and not to harm you, plans to give you hope and a future'" (Jeremiah 29:11). Hope. Confident expectation. Whether your life will include marriage or not, only God knows, but you can walk on with hope knowing that He will provide for all your needs.

Over the years I have learned that when a relationship ends, God is not *withholding* something good, He is *protecting* me and saving me from wrong choices in men.

As I look back over some of the men I've liked over the years, in the relationships that didn't work out I can see God's protective hand at work. Despite my foolishness and naïveté at times, He has kept me from harm—and from marrying the wrong person. Connor, for instance, was a nice-looking professional man whom I only dated a few times, but months later I learned that he'd committed a white-collar crime and was on his way to prison.

NEW BEGINNINGS

When love ends, it is not the end of all love in your life. It's important to remember that there are many other types of love available besides the love of a man. You may have lost *eros* love (romantic love), but you still have people in your life with whom you can give and receive *phileo* (friendship) love, like family, friends, coworkers, church members, people in ministries you belong to, hobby groups or sports teams, and others. You also have God's never-ending *agape* love. And that is everything.

WHEN LOVE ENDS,
it is not the end of
all love in your life.

Despite the darkness, morning always comes. Even on days when the sun's rays are blocked by clouds, they're still there. You just can't see them. Obstacles will come in your love life, too, and there will be days when you cannot see the way. But God's truth remains steady and true, even when you cannot see or feel it.

Beginnings from endings. Changes and choices. A wise friend once told me, "Everything is a choice, so choose wisely." The choices in your future are up to you. With God's power and presence, you can move forward with hope and confidence. It's a brand-new day!

PRAYER

Lord, Thank You for the light of day to help me see Your truth. I come to You today humbled, broken, and repentant. I'm sorry for flirting with disaster and making unwise choices in my romantic relationships. I don't want to live a life of compromise and foolishness. I ask for Your forgiveness. Thank You that Your grace covers me. It is complete and total, washing away the sin and shame, the hurt and pain. Fill me with Your love, comfort, and healing. Help me to live today in freedom and peace because of what You have done for me. Would You teach me how to love again and make healthier choices with the opposite sex? Show me what real love is—Your love—and one day, may Your love be manifested in the man You have for me. My special someone. I choose to trust You. In Jesus' name, Amen.

LIGHT FOR THE JOURNEY

I. Make a list of the men you've dated along with what you liked about each one, what you didn't like, and what you may want to consider doing differently in your next relationship. *For example:*

Theo—I liked the fact that he was athletic because I enjoy sports, too. I didn't like the fact that he watched football all day every single weekend of the season. I need someone who will be more balanced and do things I enjoy, too.

Cody—I liked that we could talk for hours and had so much in common. I didn't like the fact that he was selfish and often inconsiderate. I want a man who will honor me, respect me, and treat me like a godly woman.

James—I was attracted to him physically and to his deep spiritual walk with God. I didn't like that he wouldn't make a commitment to me. I need a man who wants to pursue dating into a lifelong marriage relationship, not just "play house."

2. Dare to imagine that things could be different in your dating life. Think about and write down specific things you envision in your next relationship (i.e., things you will do, ways you might feel, things you could see doing together as a couple). It's for your eyes only; no one else will see it so it doesn't have to be perfect. For example, "I envision myself feeling happy with the next person I choose to date. I see us laughing a lot. We talk easily

about everything, including spiritual things, because we both have a sense of humor and we like to have fun." Or, "I can see us serving together at the soup kitchen before we go to our holiday meal with family or friends. Helping others is important to me."

ILLUMINATION

I. What are some things you've learned from past relationships—things you want to stop doing? Things you want to start doing? Things you did well?

2. What are the 5Cs, essential traits to look for in a dating relationship or marriage partner?

3. What are some specific qualities you want in a boyfriend or potential husband?

4. Why are boundaries (physical and emotional) so important?

12 Brighter Days Ahead: Living in the Light

I'll tell you how the sun rose—a ribbon at a time.
—Emily Dickinson

Satisfy us in the morning with your unfailing love,
that we may sing for joy and be glad all our days.
—Psalm 90:14

Isn't it good to know that day always follows night? That winter's icy blasts always give way to the freshness of spring? Joy comes after sorrow. You've come a long way on your heart-healing journey from breaking up to brighter days ahead.

In the darkness you were *releasing*—grieving losses, healing emotional pain, and discovering the power of forgiveness as you learned to experience God's love in deeper ways.

In the dawn you were *renewing*—learning to wait well, awakening hope, and restoring your confidence and self-esteem, knowing that you really are worth being loved well.

Now it is day, and you are *restoring*—waking up to the rest of your life, finding purpose and vision, and learning to make healthier choices in relationships next time.

Healing is coming and bit by bit, you're not so affected by the breakup anymore. Even the shape of your life is changing. The physician-poet Oliver Wendell Holmes once said, "The mind, once expanded to the dimensions of larger ideas, never returns to its original size." I believe the same is true of love. The heart, once expanded to encompass the breadth of love, is never the same again.

You have changed. And, like regrowth comes after a forest fire, restoration comes after a breakup too. Ruin can be restored. Your past will always be a part of who you are; history happened. But as you walk forward by faith, you discover new companions, like inner strength and unexpected joy. Hope arises. Things start to get better.

Surprisingly, the human heart is quite flexible and resilient; it has the ability to bounce back from difficulties. But you're really not bouncing "back," you're bouncing forward—from darkness to light, deadness to life, brokenness to greater wholeness, fear to courage, and so much more. God is all about transformation. "I will guide you," He says in Isaiah 42:16, "I will turn the darkness into light before them and make the rough places smooth."

> # YOU'RE NOT BOUNCING
> "back," you're bouncing forward—from darkness to light, deadness to life, brokenness to greater wholeness, fear to courage, and so much more.

It's time to live in the light.

WHAT'S BLOCKING THE LIGHT IN YOUR LIFE?

Walking in the light means you are choosing to follow Jesus Christ, the Light, with a capital L. He is the One who brings truth into deceived and darkened hearts. Jesus said, "I am the light of the world. Whoever follows me will never walk in darkness, but will have the light of life" (John 8:12).

When we receive Jesus into our own lives, He lives in us so we become more like Him. He tells us that *we* are to shine that light—to be Christ-like and share it with the rest of the world so others can praise God too.

You are the light of the world. A city on a hill cannot be hidden. Neither do people light a lamp and put it under a bowl. Instead they put it on its stand, and it gives light to everyone in the house. In the same way, let your light shine before men, that they may see your good deeds and praise your Father in heaven. (Matthew 5:14–16)

Does that mean we are perfect or that we never fail? No. God knows we are human, He created us. It means that we are Christ-followers, faithful as best we can be to His words and actions, with a heart toward obedience, integrity, and love.

But sometimes we feel anything but radiant. We want to be like "a city on a hill," but something or someone snuffs out our light. They put a bowl over our brilliance to keep us from shining.

What keeps us from being victorious? What blocks the light in our lives?

First, we know that the Evil One wants to frustrate and foil our plans and bring our lives utter ruin. That could be a part of the blockage. Other things that can block our radiance are things we hide, like sin (Isaiah 29:15–16), wrong motives, fear, shame, feelings of unworthiness, ignorance, or we are simply darkened in our understanding.

One of the biggest traps that trips us up and keeps us in the dark is comparison. I've heard women jealously bemoan the fact that their friends have boyfriends or husbands and they don't, and it eats them up inside. "Well, she's on her second marriage and I've never even been married once," they may say, or "She has a husband and kids and she never had to work outside the home; I'm single and I work all the time—it's not fair." Wondering when love will come for you is one thing, being envious is another.

Maybe you're having a hard time accepting that this breakup really happened. You want to be in the Day, moving forward with your life and having hope, but you are still bitter and holding on to what you "should've had." Unlike the board game LIFE, where the path winds through life events like graduation, jobs, marriage, kids, and retirement, you never got your little red convertible filled up with a husband in the seat next to yours, and a bunch of kids in the back.

No matter what your situation, God is still sovereign. Just because the road of real life took a different turn, does not mean God has forgotten about you. He is still with you on the path.

"The sovereign Lord will not be thwarted by ill motives, wayward plans, or the scheming of the unrighteous. He rules over the universe, and he even uses evil to accomplish his plan," says Dan Allender. "But God's sovereignty is not an invitation to passivity. Instead, it is a call to wise and risky creativity. We must plan, and he will direct."[1] God can use anything to get you on the right road and keep you there, even a breakup.

You want to live in the light, and stay on God's path, but how?

HOW TO LIVE IN THE LIGHT

Living in the light doesn't mean your path is sunshine and blue skies every day. It means that whether your day is full of emotional darkness or cheerful calm, you stay focused forward, reading and absorbing God's truth from the Word. As you do, you experience new aspects of God's character. Faith increases and, over time, you begin to find victory; you are less fearful and more confident. You know you will be okay with or without a man in your life. You believe that God has the power to handle your pain and help you make wiser choices in love.

Instead of a darkened heart that wants to go backwards, you choose to *walk forward by faith*. You know that hard times may come again, but you don't avoid them. You go through, knowing the struggle will strengthen you, build character, and bring you one step closer to better days.

Because you've been in the dark times, the hard times, you can appreciate and celebrate the good. "There is no victory unless a battle is waged. There is no one who overcomes unless obstacles are hurdled," said Marsha Crockett in *Dancing in the Desert*.

"We want Easter joy without Good Friday sorrow," she continues, "We want Christmas cheer without the dark, damp manger. We want the Good Shepherd but not the wounded Lamb of God."[2]

Because of Easter joy, we can have hope. To the world, once dark and dead, Jesus Christ brought light and life. Ephesians 5:8 says, "For you were once darkness, but now you are light in the Lord. Live as children of light." To live as children of light we need to:

Push back the darkness. When the Evil One tries to snuff out your joy and turn your 100-watt life into a blackout, push back the darkness. Stand in your authority. Pray in the power of the Holy Spirit. Power up! With the armor of God you can not only stand strong but advance. Ephesians 6:10–18 (emphasis mine) reads,

> Finally, be strong in the Lord and in his mighty power. Put on the full armor of God so that you can take your stand against the devil's schemes. For our struggle is not against flesh and blood, but against the rulers, against the authorities, against the powers of this dark world and against the spiritual forces of evil in the heavenly realms. Therefore put on the full armor of God, so that when the day of evil comes, you may be able to stand your ground, and after you have done everything, to stand. Stand firm then, with the *belt of truth* buckled around your waist, with the *breastplate of righteousness* in place, and with your feet fitted with the readiness that comes from *the gospel of peace.* In addition to all this, take up the *shield of faith,* with which you can extinguish all the flaming arrows of the evil one. Take the *helmet of salvation* and the *sword of the Spirit,* which is the word of God. And pray in the Spirit on all occasions with all kinds of prayers and requests.

Focus forward. Stay on the path *toward God,* moving increasingly forward as you trust the One who has been completely faithful through the twilight, night, dawn, and day. We often grapple with thinking our way is best, and that the "My Way" Highway is the right way. With stubborn pride, ignorance, and selfish ways we miss God's yield sign—or worse, blast past the "Road Closed" warning—and end up on a dead-end street or in a wreck. Proverbs 4:25–27 says, "Let your eyes look straight ahead, fix your gaze directly before you. Make level paths for your feet and take only ways that are firm. Do not swerve to the right or the left; keep your foot from evil."

Love extravagantly. As you begin to absorb more of God's unconditional love for you, it enables you to better love yourself and love others. "Love one another deeply, from the heart" (1 Peter 1:22). Be a giver, not a taker. Find out what makes the other person happy and do special things for him—even little things.

> NO MATTER WHAT your marital status, you can share the love you have with everyone, especially those in need.

When conflict comes, care enough to talk about issues and not avoid them. Show the other person how you feel and tell them. You can say "I love you" with words and actions—whether it's giving a hug or giving your attention after a long day at work. A kind act goes a long way.

Thankfully, Gary Chapman has shared his wisdom on how people express and receive love in different ways in his bestselling book *The Five Love Languages*. Each person has one or more of these five love languages—ways to meet each other's deepest emotional needs: words of affirmation, quality time, receiving gifts, acts of service, or physical touch.[3] Find out what each of you needs and then you can each demonstrate love and receive love in the ways that are most meaningful to you.

God's commandments to love one another are not reserved for just a special man in your life. No matter what your marital status, you can share the love you have with everyone, especially those in need. One man I know carries gift certificates with him for local fast-food restaurants and when he sees a homeless person, he gives them away. Love bravely. Love courageously.

Share your light with others. Because the light of Christ lives in you, you shine, and you can share that radiance—that hope—with others still in darkness. Sharing your light doesn't always mean you have to share your salvation story—although that is a good thing. You can also pass on the light of Christ to others as you show mercy, grant forgiveness, and lend a listening ear to someone who is lonely.

Don't hide your light. Share it. You can be a woman of influence and impact even with the little you have, just as the light of one single candle can make a difference.

Perhaps your church, like ours, has a candle-lighting time on Christmas Eve, when the houselights are lowered and the pastor lights one candle. From his starter candle, one person lights another's and another's until finally the entire room is filled with the quiet, yet powerful, glow of hundreds of lit candles.

Likewise, the light from one single person, when given away, can light up the world—whether it's right in your neighborhood or across the globe.

Celebrate what God has done for you. "I sought the Lord, and he answered me; he delivered me from all my fears. Those who look to him are *radiant*; their faces are never covered with shame" (Psalm 34:4–5, emphasis mine). Look what God has done. Change is coming, and has come. You may not see it, but often others do; they see a difference in your countenance as you get farther from the land of loss and deeper into the delight of a new day. You begin to have a lighter heart and a sunnier countenance. You seem happier. So celebrate all He has done for you in this journey. Enjoy God. Enjoy your life.

As you learn to live in the light by pushing back the darkness, focusing forward, loving extravagantly, sharing your light with others, and celebrating what God has done for you, remember that this path of life continues. It leads into your future, and into another day—one without an end.

ANTICIPATE THE BIG DAY

Nope, it's not your wedding day (although that will be an important day in your life); the big day to come is when Jesus returns and there is no more night. Envision it: no more heartache, no more pain, no fear or worry, disease or death. "He will wipe every tear from their eyes. There will be no more death or mourning or crying or pain, for the old order of things has passed away" (Revelation 21:4).

No more darkness. When that day comes, you won't need a night-light or a flashlight to see in the dark, not even the sun. "There will be no more night. They will not need the light of a lamp or the light of the sun, for the Lord God will give them light. And they will reign for ever and ever" (Revelation 22:5).

Whether it happens in one single day or over a period of time is debated. What we do know is that when Jesus left the earth He promised to return. He is coming back. That is our hope; that is our solid promise. What a glorious day it will be when we see Him in the clouds (Revelation 1:7), the Lord God, the One "who is, and who was, and who is to come, the Almighty" (Revelation 1:8).

The good news is that we know how the story ends. God wins; we win! In the end, God makes all things right. He restores and He reveals. We will get to see clearly the face of God, not the unambiguous, distorted image you see when the bathroom mirror fogs up, but clearly and face-to-face. "Now we see but a poor reflection as in a mirror; then we shall see face to face. Now I know in part; then I shall know fully, even as I am fully known" (1 Corinthians 13:12). Can you imagine? Fully known and fully loved.

You don't have to wait until the Lord returns for your heart restoration. He is even now in the process of rebuilding and restoring your broken heart and shattered dreams.

All will be restored. One day.
Until then, live in the light. And keep on walking.

THE BEST DAYS ARE AHEAD

To me, it is a mystery and a miracle how two people ever get together and stay together. Thankfully, the God we serve is really good at mysteries and miracles. And He excels at new beginnings.

Throughout your heart-healing journey you have become more equipped, empowered, and encouraged to move forward in your life. Remember what you learned in the dark. Total dependence on God, day and night, night and day. He is the God of unlimited wisdom, tender mercies, awesome power, and unfailing love. "For this God is our God for ever and ever; he will be our guide even to the end" (Psalm 48:14). The best days are ahead.

Lead on Lord, lead on.

Lord, thank You for bringing me through this breakup. Thank You for restoration. We have come a long way and I am so grateful. I want to live in the light and be more like You. Will You lift whatever is blocking the light of Christ from shining brighter in my life? I choose to walk forward by faith, toward You. With joyful anticipation I long for the day I will see You face-to-face. What a day it will be! Equipped, empowered, and encouraged, let Your light shine in me so I can be a radiant woman every day. In Jesus' name, Amen.

ILLUMINATION

1. Think about the sentence, "Don't forget in the light what you learned in the dark." What does that mean to you?

2. Based on the passage Matthew 5:14–16, what seems to be blocking the light from shining in your life?

3. What are one or two things you can do this week to "live in the light"?

4. Because Christ lives in you, shine. How can you share the light (the truth and insight you've received) with someone else to make a difference in their life?

Notes

Chapter 2: The Edge of Evening: Getting Comfort and Support

1. Alicia Britt Chole, *Anonymous: Jesus' Hidden Years . . . and Yours* (Franklin, Tenn.: Integrity Publishers, 2006), 61.
2. Eugene Peterson, *A Message of Comfort & Hope* (Nashville: J. Countryman, a division of Thomas Nelson, 2005), 80.
3. http://www.columbia.edu/itc/cerc/seeu/bio2/restrict/modules/module 09_content.html.

Chapter 3: Nightfall: Grieving Losses

1. John W. James and Russell Friedman, *The Grief Recovery Handbook* (New York: Harper Perennial, a division of HarperCollins Publishers, 1998), back cover.
2. Ibid., 3.
3. Ibid.
4. Gary R. Collins, Ph.D., *Christian Counseling: A Comprehensive Guide* (Dallas: Word Publishing, 1988), 351.
5. Ibid., 350.
6. Tim Baker, *Broken* (Colorado Springs: NavPress, 2006), 142.
7. Ibid.
8. Ibid., 144.

Chapter 4: The Midnight Hour: Healing Emotional Pain

1. Dr. Steve Stephens and Pam Vredevelt, *The Wounded Women* (Sisters, Ore.: Multnomah Publishers, 2006), 30.
2. Ibid.
3. Ibid.
4. John Eldredge, *Desire* (Nashville: Thomas Nelson, 2000 and 2007), 73.

Chapter 5: Night Lights: Experiencing God's Love

1. Anne Graham Lotz, *Why?* (Nashville: W Publishing Group, a division of Thomas Nelson Publishers, 2004), 71.
2. C. J. Mahaney, *The Cross Centered Life* (Sisters, Ore.: Multnomah Publishers, Inc., 2002), 47.

3. Max Lucado, *Traveling Light Journal* (Nashville: W Publishing Group, a division of Thomas Nelson, 2001), 31.

4. Jackie M. Johnson, *Power Prayers for Women* (Uhrichsville, Ohio: Barbour Publishing, 2007), 8.

Chapter 6: Out of the Shadows: Discovering the Power of Forgiveness

1. Henri J. M. Nouwen, *Life of the Beloved* (New York: The Crossroad Publishing Company, 1992), 61.

2. Neil T. Anderson, *Victory Over the Darkness* (Ventura, Calif.: Regal Books, 2000, Second Edition), 185.

3. Ibid., 185.

4. Ibid., 187.

5. Ibid., 188.

6. Dan Allender and Tremper Longman III, *Bold Love* (Colorado Springs: WaterBrook Press, 1999), 88.

7. C. D. Baker, *40 Loaves: Breaking Bread with Our Father Each Day* (Colorado Springs: WaterBrook Press, 2009), 145.

8. John Bevere, *The Bait of Satan* (Lake Mary, Fla.: Charisma House, 2004), 8.

9. Ibid., 163.

10. Henri J. M. Nouwen, *The Return of the Prodigal Son* (New York: Image Books/Doubleday, 1992), 53.

11. Robert Jeffress, *When Forgiveness Doesn't Make Sense* (Colorado Springs: WaterBrook Press, 2000), 33.

12. Allender and Longman, *Bold Love*, 162.

13. Ibid., 162–63.

Chapter 7: Before Sunrise: Learning to Wait Well

1. Jerome Daley, *When God Waits* (Colorado Springs: WaterBrook Press, 2005), 61.

2. http://www.famousquotesandauthors.com/authors/e__m__bounds_quotes.html.

3. Mark Buchanan, *The Rest of God: Restoring Your Soul by Restoring Sabbath* (Nashville: W Publishing Group, a division of Thomas Nelson, 2006), 61.

4. Dan B. Allender, *The Healing Path* (Colorado Springs: WaterBrook Press, 1999), 40.

Chapter 8: First Light: Awakening Hope

1. Eugene H. Peterson, *A Message of Comfort and Hope* (Nashville: J. Countryman, a division of Thomas Nelson, 2005), 57.

2. Larry Crabb, *Shattered Dreams* (Colorado Springs: WaterBrook Press, 2001), 62.

3. Judith Couchman, *The Shadow of His Hand* (Colorado Springs: WaterBrook Press, 2002), 33.

Chapter 9: Illumination: Restoring Confidence and Self-Esteem

1. Jud Wilhite with Bill Taaffe, *Eyes Wide Open* (Colorado Springs: Multnomah Books, 2009), x.
2. Ibid., xi.
3. Lisa Bevere, *The True Measure of a Woman* (Lake Mary, Fla.: Charisma House, 1997, 2007), 118.
4. William Backus and Marie Chapian, *Telling Yourself the Truth* (Minneapolis: Bethany House Publishers, 1980), 21.
5. Neil T. Anderson, *The Bondage Breaker* (Eugene, Oregon: Harvest House Publishers, 2000), 51.
6. Ibid., 51–52.
7. John and Stasi Eldredge, *Captivating* (Nashville: Thomas Nelson, 2005), 152.
8. Ibid., 153.
9. Nancy Leigh DeMoss, *Brokenness* (Chicago: Moody Publishers, 2002), 131.
10. Dr. Henry Cloud, *Changes That Heal* (Grand Rapids: Zondervan Publishing House, 1990, 1992), 45.
11. Ibid., 110.

Chapter 10: Arise: Waking Up to the Rest of Your Life

1. Henri J. M. Nouwen, *The Return of the Prodigal Son* (New York: Image Books, 1994), 86.

Chapter 11: Shine: Making Healthier Choices Next Time

1. Dr. Kevin Leman, *Pleasers* (Grand Rapids: Revell, 2006), 105.
2. Bill and Lynne Hybels' thoughts in *Fit To Be Tied* (Grand Rapids: Zondervan Publishing House, 1991) have helped to form my ideas on this topic.
3. Stephen Arterburn and Dr. Meg J. Rinck, *Finding Mr. Right* (Nashville: Thomas Nelson, 2001), 77.
4. Michelle McKinney Hammond and Joel A. Brooks Jr., *The Unspoken Rules of Love* (Colorado Springs: WaterBrook Press, 2003), 73.
5. Ibid., 73.
6. Bill and Lynne Hybels, *Fit To Be Tied*, 75.
7. Biblical Dating: Just Friends, Scott Croft (Boundless.org website, 2005), http://www.boundless.org/2005/articles/a0001475.cfm.
8. Dr. Henry Cloud and Dr. John Townsend, *Boundaries* (Grand Rapids: Zondervan Publishing House, 1992), 31.
9. Susie Larson, *The Uncommon Woman* (Chicago: Moody Publishers, 2008), 166.

Chapter 12: Brighter Days Ahead: Living in the Light

1. Dan B. Allender, *To Be Told* (Colorado Springs: WaterBrook Press, 2005), 113.
2. Marsha Crockett, *Dancing in the Desert* (Downer's Grove, Ill.: InterVarsity Press, 2003), 109.
3. Gary Chapman, *The Five Love Languages* (Chicago: Northfield Publishing, 1992, 1995, 2010), 38. (www.5lovelanguages.com)

Acknowledgments

Writing a book is a collaborative effort, and I would like to heartily thank:

- Joel Kneedler at Alive Communications for his guidance, insight, and indispensable sense of humor.
- Steve Lyon and the staff at Moody Publishers for their hard work—ability with affability—and belief in the message of this book to heal hearts and change lives.
- Jocelyn Green, my developmental editor, whose sharp editorial knife trimmed the fat from the manuscript but left enough for it to still taste good. You did an excellent job. Thank you.
- My friends, family, and the *When Love Ends* prayer team for your encouragement, support, prayers, and random acts of sustenance (thank you, Maria and Bobby) over the months of writing. I couldn't have done it without you!

+ Friends who kindly and enthusiastically read chapter drafts and gave input to make this a stronger and better book: Anne Caddell, Judy Downing, Sue Eilertsen, Barbara Lynch, and Maribeth Sacho. Your efforts—and friendship—are much appreciated.

+ Everyone who contributed their personal stories to this book. I am grateful. May the words you've shared help others to be encouraged and inspired.

+ The One who loves me most, Jesus Christ: for opening doors, for really good ideas, and for sustaining me through breakups and new beginnings. *May Your presence be on every page.*

About the Author

JACKIE M. JOHNSON's first book, *Power Prayers for Women,* has sold nearly 150,000 copies. She has also written articles, poetry, and hundreds of devotionals for Focus on the Family's *Renewing the Heart* website. A native of Milwaukee, Jackie lives in Colorado Springs, Colorado. Visit her encouragement blog, A New Day Café, at anewdaycafe.blogspot.com or her website, www.jackiejohnsoncreative.com.

I KISSED A LOT OF FROGS

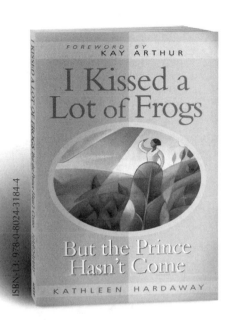

ISBN-13: 978-0-8024-3184-4

A single's guide for abundant life in Christ. Often singles in the church feel overlooked. Additionally, so many resources are aimed at helping singles prepare for and find mates. Kathleen Hardaway offers *I Kissed A Lot of Frogs* as an indispensable alternative pointing singles to Jesus for their joy, their strength, and their completeness. Sharing her own journey from heartbreak and disappointment to wholeness and contentment, Hardaway helps readers get and stay focused on the perfect plan God has for their lives.